P9-APA-742

THE WAYS OF LANGUAGE

A READER

COMPLIMENTS OF

THE ODYSSEY PRESS · INC ·

55 FIFTH AVENUE   NEW YORK 10003

The Ways
of Language

A Reader

Edited by

RAYMOND J. PFLUG

College of San Mateo

THE ODYSSEY PRESS, INC.

NEW YORK

DISCARDED

LORETTE WILMOT LIBRARY
NAZARETH COLLEGE

© Copyright 1967 by The Odyssey Press, Inc.

All Rights Reserved   Printed in the United States

Library of Congress Catalog Card Number: 66-26108

A 0 9 8 7 6 5 4 3 2 1

208585

ACKNOWLEDGMENTS

The author wishes to thank the following authors, agents, and publishers for permission to reprint copyrighted material.

Mortimer Adler – for "How to Read A Dictionary." Reprinted by permission of the author.

Maxwell Aley Associates – for "Who Flang That Ball," by W. F. Miksch. Reprinted by permission of the author's agent.

Appleton-Century-Crofts – for "The Enrichment of the Language During the Renaissance," by Albert C. Baugh. From *A History of the English Language,* 2nd edition, by Albert C. Baugh. Copyright © 1957 by Appleton-Century-Crofts, Inc. Reprinted by permission of the publishers.

Edgar Dale – for "Clear Only If Known," by Edgar Dale. Reprinted by permission of the author.

Bergen Evans – for "But What's a Dictionary For?" by Bergen Evans. Reprinted by permission of the author.

Margaret Follett – for "Sabotage in Springfield," by Wilson Follett. Reprinted by permission of Mrs. Follett.

Alice Hamilton – for "English Is a Queer Language," by Alice Hamilton, M.D. Reprinted by permission of the author.

Harcourt, Brace & World, Inc. – for "Gobbledygook," by Stuart Chase. From *The Power of Words,* copyright, 1953, 1954, by Stuart Chase. Reprinted by permission of Harcourt, Brace & World, Inc.

Harper & Row, Publishers, Incorporated – for "They Talk Past Each Other," from *How To Talk With People* by Irving J. Lee. Copyright 1952 by Harper & Brothers. Reprinted by permission of Harper & Row, Publishers.

Donald Lloyd – for "Our National Mania for Correctness," by Donald Lloyd. Reprinted by permission of the author.

808.04271
PSI

National Council of Teachers of English – for "The Freshman and His Dictionary" by Mitford M. Mathews from CCC for December, 1955. Reprinted with the permission of the National Council of Teachers of English and Mitford M. Mathews.

The New York Times – for "Ugly Words," by J. Donald Adams; "Sound and Sense of Words," by John P. Sisk; "More on Ugly Words," by J. Donald Adams; "About: New Words," by Martin Tolchin; "Webster's New Word Book," by Norman E. Isaacs; and "Two Journals Score New Dictionary," by Foster Hailey. All copyright by The New York Times. Reprinted by permission.

The New Yorker – for "Morning Exercises," by Robert M. Coates, © 1960 The New Yorker Magazine, Inc., reprinted by permission; for excerpts from "Our Own Modern English Usage," by James Thurber, Copr. © 1929, 1957 The New Yorker Magazine, Inc. Reprinted by permission.

John P. Sisk – for "Sound and Sense of Words," by John P. Sisk. Reprinted by permission of the author.

This Week Magazine – for "Who Flang That Ball," by W. F. Miksch. Reprinted from *This Week* Magazine. Copyright 1951 by the United Newspaper Magazine Corporation.

The University of North Carolina Press – for "Can You Understand the Rules of Federal Prose," by James R. Masterson and Wendell Brooks Phillips. From *Federal Prose* by Masterson and Phillips. Reprinted by permission.

The University Press of Virginia – for "Session Eight, March 13, 1958," from *Faulkner in the University*, edited by Frederick L. Gwynn and Joseph L. Blotner.

The Viking Press – for excerpts from interviews with Truman Capote and Frank O'Connor. From *Writers at Work*, edited by Malcolm Cowley, copyright © 1957, 1958 by The Paris Review, Inc. Reprinted by permission of The Viking Press, Inc.

The Washington Post – for "Keep Your Old Webster's," an editorial by The Washington Post. Reprinted by permission.

Cora Chase Williamson – for "How to Write Like a Social Scientist," by Samuel T. Williamson. Reprinted by permission.

The World Publishing Company – for "Ernest Hemingway," by Harvey Breit. Reprinted by permission of The World Publishing Company from *The Writer Observed* by Harvey Breit. Copyright © 1956 by Harvey Breit. For "English: His Sisters, His Cousins, His Aunts," by Charlton Laird, reprinted by permission of The World Publishing Company from *The Miracle of Language* by Charlton Laird. Copyright © 1953 by Charlton Laird.

Preface

This book is based on two assumptions: (1) English teachers know more about and have more training and experience in the English language than in psychology or sociology, politics or athletics. (2) People, including students, are naturally curious about their language; an otherwise lifeless class will wake up to a discussion of borrowings, dialects, and coinages. All the readings in this book, then, are about language and the ways it works.

Short introductions have been supplied for each section, and most selections are followed by discussions. For vocabulary study, where desired, explanations of some of the words used in the readings are at the end of the book. Inasmuch as the definitions are intended as reading aids, they apply to the words as used in the selections and consequently are not to be taken as complete definitions. Some of the allusions are also briefly explained. The discussions can be used by the student for review purposes and for writing assignments.

One hopes, of course, that the book will be found to be complete in itself, but consideration has also been given to its possible integration with other texts. For example, it can be used in conjunction with a conventional workbook, supplying broader subject matter. The section entitled "Writers on Writing," containing interviews with Faulkner, Hemingway, Capote, and O'Connor, might well lead to further reading of works by those authors. The section entitled "The Word-Hoard" might introduce a unit on dictionary study. However the book is used, the readings will help students to become more fully aware of the ways in which their own language works.

Contents

1. Words Used, Misused, and Abused   1

UGLY WORDS J. Donald Adams   2
SOUND AND SENSE OF WORDS John P. Sisk   5
MORE ON UGLY WORDS J. Donald Adams   10

2. On the Background of Your Language   13

ENGLISH: HIS SISTERS, HIS COUSINS, HIS AUNTS
     Charlton Laird   14
THE ENRICHMENT OF THE LANGUAGE DURING
     THE RENAISSANCE Albert C. Baugh   19

3. Vocabulary   23

MORNING EXERCISES Robert M. Coates   24
ENGLISH IS A QUEER LANGUAGE
     Alice Hamilton, M.D.   29
THEY TALK PAST EACH OTHER Irving Lee   33
ABOUT: NEW WORDS Martin Tolchin   44

4. The Word-Hoard   47

THE FRESHMAN AND HIS DICTIONARY
     Mitford M. Mathews   49
HOW TO READ A DICTIONARY Mortimer Adler   56
SABOTAGE IN SPRINGFIELD Wilson Follett   66
BUT WHAT'S A DICTIONARY FOR? Bergen Evans   77
WEBSTER'S NEW WORD BOOK Norman E. Isaacs   91
KEEP YOUR OLD WEBSTER'S The Washington Post   93
TWO JOURNALS SCORE NEW DICTIONARY
     Foster Hailey   95

5. The Language Exploited and Exploded and
    Occasionally Exuberated and Extravagated   96

    GOBBLEDYGOOK   Stuart Chase   98
    HOW TO WRITE LIKE A SOCIAL SCIENTIST
        Samuel T. Williamson   109
    CAN YOU UNDERSTAND THE RULES OF FEDERAL PROSE?
        James R. Masterson and
                Wendell Brooks Phillips   115
    WHO FLANG THAT BALL   W. F. Miksch   124

6. Advice on How to Write   128

    OUR NATIONAL MANIA FOR CORRECTNESS
        Donald J. Lloyd   129
    CLEAR ONLY IF KNOWN   Edgar Dale   136
    LADIES' AND GENTLEMEN'S GUIDE TO MODERN
        ENGLISH USAGE   James Thurber   142

7. Writers on Writing   149

    FAULKNER IN THE UNIVERSITY   Edited by
        Frederick L. Gwynn and Joseph L. Blotner   150
    ERNEST HEMINGWAY   Harvey Breit   163
    TRUMAN CAPOTE   The Paris Review   166
    FRANK O'CONNOR   The Paris Review   168

Vocabulary Study   171

THE WAYS OF LANGUAGE

A READER

1

Words Used, Misused, and Abused

THE FOLLOWING READINGS are about words. We are so accustomed to using words as vehicles for conveying whatever we have to say that we are likely never to give much thought to the words as words. Words are but containers, and who pays much attention to the box? We are more concerned about what is in the box.

In the first selection J. Donald Adams, a well-known editor and critic, writes about words he calls hideous, words like "beautician" and "funeral home"; the last one he labels a verbal absurdity. Professor John Sisk differs with Adams, arguing that words can be neither hideous nor beautiful in themselves; it all depends on how they are used. In the third selection Adams is heard in rebuttal. We observe two men in disagreement, and their verbal exchange seems not to affect either one.

As you read, try to decide whether you are on the side of Adams or of Sisk; then attempt to determine what causes your choice. Does the writer you choose express one of your opinions for you? Does he appeal to some prejudice? Does he use some device, some technique particularly effective with you?

Ugly Words

J. DONALD ADAMS

Some time ago, in response to a query, I gave over this column to a discussion of what might be considered the most beautiful line in the English language. The other day, reading Eric Barnes' moving biography of Edward Sheldon, *The Man Who Lived Twice*, I came upon a passage in which Mr. Barnes tells how Sheldon, in company with his oculist, Dr. Doherty, once amused himself by conjuring up "the most hideous words in the English language." Together, they concluded that no such list would be complete without the inclusion of "intelligentsia," "funeral parlor," "housewife," and "galluses."

For the most part, these seem to me relatively inoffensive words. "Intelligentsia," to be sure, carries with it a faint tinge of snobbishness, and is, to my mind, definitely unprecise in its connotations, in view of the fact that intelligence and education are by no means interchangeable terms. To call it hideous, however, strikes me as exaggerated. In fact, none of the words which Ned Sheldon and his medical friend found so obnoxious seems to me acutely distasteful, with the exception of "funeral parlor," which carries nice-nellieism to the nth degree. I find nothing to recommend the use, now so prevalent, of the phrase "funeral home," which is unquestionably one of the ultimates in verbal absurdity. It now disfigures the streets of every American town and city. "Housewife," on the other hand, while by no means a glamorous or exciting word, is in my estimate an honest and inoffensive one. And "galluses," I think, wears a humorous and stoutly homespun air. It has a lot more flavor than "suspenders"; as for "braces," that strikes me as a merely inaccurate word.

Even though I cannot subscribe to Sheldon's verbal antipathetics, I am grateful to him for channeling my thoughts, however briefly, in this direction. Unfortunately, for my purpose, some of the most hideous words in the English language cannot be printed in a newspaper, but let's see what can be scared up that falls within the bounds of permitted usage.

Suppose we stop to consider what the qualities are that justify the adjective "hideous" as applied to that decidedly living organism, the word. Those qualities must vary considerably in kind and degree, depending upon the temperament and tastes, the susceptibilities of the person exposed to them. In my own case, I should place first on the list of such qualities, that of disagreeable sound. None of Sheldon's strong aversions seem to me indictable for that reason. All his hated words come smoothly to the tongue, nor do they grate upon the ear. They are not beautiful, or even pretty; they are innocuous so far as euphony goes, though the hissing of "galluses" is no asset. And "intelligentsia," as a matter of fact, has a rather rippling sound. The other quality which merits the application of hideous is the power of a word to evoke disgusting or otherwise extremely repellent sensations.

What nominations, then, might we make of words truly deserving the designation hideous, leaving out of account such words as are offensive to many readers? This narrows our choice, of course, but it should be possible to find a few which are hideous without inducing queasiness. The choice could be more easily made if the words could be taken from certain of the American Indian tongues —beautiful as some Indian words and names are—or from German. *Schrecklichkeit,* for example, or, for that matter, pleasant as its connotations are, *gesundheit.* Even French, the aristocrat of languages, yields a few such distasteful words. *Crépuscule* beloved though it is by many poets, when adopted into English as the adjective "crepuscular," certainly makes a bid for election.

For a mildly hideous word, there is "polygamous." Attractive as it may be in its connotations, it is certainly not auditorily entrancing. "Pneumococcus" is a likely candidate, as are other words denoting those pestiferous small organisms which make continual war on us. A special niche might be reserved for words like "mortician" and "beautician," and another special compartment for such verbal contraptions as "snaggletoothed."

A little worse, I think, than these, is a word that stands for love-liness—"pulchritudinous." If you were Marilyn Monroe and did not know English very well, and someone called you that, would you think you were being complimented? Then there is a word which, not so many years ago, enjoyed a brief vogue among book reviewers, and which has always seemed to me to reach the sum-mit of clumsiness. I refer to "adumbrate," meaning to sketch an outline in a shadowy way. (Now the great vogue word is, and has been for some time, "perceptive," to which no exception can be taken, save on grounds of overuse.)

"Pococurantism" is to me definitely a hideous word. I had never seen it until I began leafing the dictionary in search of horrible examples. I doubt that it is ever used, like a lot of other top-heavy Latinities, but it means the attitude or behaviour characteristic of a person who may be more briefly and euphoniously described as a trifler. I leave you to compile a list salted to your own taste.

DISCUSSION

Do you consider any words hideous? Why? Do you object to their meaning, their connotation, or their sound? To test your reaction, try to find other words to express the same thing and see how consistent your reaction is. For example, someone might consider "ain't" hideous, but what about "faint" and "quaint"? A meat market once advertised offal for sale and some customers expressed distaste. What were they objecting to in the word? Mr. Adams dislikes "polygamous"; what about "polychrome" and "polycone"?

Consider the word "hideous" itself. Would you prefer that Adams use a different word? At one point he talks about "that decidedly living organism, the word." What does he mean? How can a word be a living organism?

Sound and Sense of Words

JOHN P. SISK

Critic J. Donald Adams devoted his New York *Times Book Review* column for September 30, 1956, to a discussion of hideous words, submitting as examples "polygamous," "pneumococcus," "mortician," "beautician," "pulchritudinous" and "pococurantism." These words and others failed to meet his requirements for verbal beauty; either they had a disagreeable sound, did not come smoothly to the tongue, or they evoked "disgusting and otherwise repellent sensations."

This sounds like the literary small-talk one ought to allow a critic to indulge himself in every now and then. But is it small-talk? Words are so important that one ought to pay close attention to all theorizing about them. Mr. Adams' speculations, I suggest, are founded on questionable assumptions that are shared by a great number of people who also believe that they love words and literature. These assumptions about the functions of words are involved with some unfortunate beliefs about all fine writing, and especially about poetry.

One of these assumptions is that the beauty or hideousness of a word can be found in the word itself, isolated or abstracted from any context. This is a dictionary approach to language.

In a dictionary words have an artificial, if very useful, kind of existence. Only in a secondary sense, does a word "mean" in a dictionary, or in any other state of isolation. A dictionary definition can be a very useful tool for clarifying words in contexts, but, like a prose comment on a poem, it is still best thought of as a clue to a semantic problem that must ultimately be worked out *in situ.* Just as an ecologist has nothing to do with organisms isolated from their biologic environments, so as normal users of language we have nothing to do with isolated words. All communication is done with words in contexts, even where, for instance in conversation, words are apparently used singly. For

5

context is not only other words; it is also time, place, circumstance, accompanying gesture, anticipated response and so on.

Similarly, the beauty in organized language is not so much the result of putting beautiful words together as it is putting words together beautifully—into Eliot's "complete consort dancing together." It is irrelevant to ask whether the words so organized are beautiful when taken singly. The gestalt formula, that the whole is greater than the sum of its parts, is the right one here. The beauty of a pattern of words is ecological, the property of words in a pattern, not of a sum of beautiful verbal moments.

Mr. Adams' first requirement for a beautiful word—that it have an agreeable sound, come smoothly to the tongue—may work well enough if one is playing parlor games with words as words, but it is useless when applied to words in contexts. What, for instance, would Mr. Adams say about "orcs" (a variety of whales)? Taken by itself, this belch-like monosyllable is hardly lovely. But hear it in the wonderful passage from Book XI of *Paradise Lost:*

> ... Then shall this Mount
> Of Paradise by might of waves be moved ...
> Down the great River to the Op'ning Gulf,
> And there take root, an Island salt and bare,
> The haunt of Seals and Orcs, and sea-mews' clang.

Equally useless is Adams' second requirement, the power of a word to evoke pleasant or beautiful sensations. Granted that the isolated word (provided that isolation is possible) may evoke some kind of sensation, still the sensations, or images, that concern us primarily are those evoked by words in patterns. If you test isolated words according to their power to evoke pleasant sensations, you are not only likely to be hopelessly subjective, but you will find out little about their real evocative potential. If Mr. Adams objects to "pulchritudinous" on this score, he might very well object to "polyphiloprogenitive," yet it goes very well in Mr. Eliot's "Sunday Morning Service":

> Polyphiloprogenitive
> The sapient sutlers of the word. ...

Or Mr. Adams might reasonably say that a word like "illimitable" is too abstract to evoke any kind of sensation—or at any rate a pleasant one. Yet Coleridge, surely a hard man to take a stand against, admired it immensely in Cullen Bryant's lines:

> The desert and illimitable air—
> Lone wandering, but not lost.

And aren't "incarnadine" and "multitudinous" perfect examples of the "top-heavy Latinities" Mr. Adams abhors? I wonder if he finds them so abhorrent in *Macbeth:*

> No, this my hand will rather
> The multitudinous seas incarnadine,
> Making the green one red.

So Mr. Adams may think he is considering the beauty or hideousness of words taken singly, but what he is really considering is words in partial, vaguely specified or purely personal contexts, from which he is no more able to tear them than any one else. His assumption, however, is that he has got them loose and that something like definitive statements about their potentialities for contexts can be made about them in this disengaged condition. Thus he can say that there is a faint tinge of snobbishness in "intelligentsia," when the snobbishness is only in contexts he is most familiar with, or has elected to favor—which are by no means all possible contexts.

Perhaps it is best to say that, unless it is unambiguously mimetic, the completely isolated word has only phonic properties—is a pattern, more or less attractive, of certain vowels, consonants, and syllabic pauses. From this point of view certainly not all words would be equally beautiful to the ideally sensitive ear. But the problem would be to hear words in one's own language this way, completely separated from all sense and context. One might as well try to be ideally objective about himself.

However, I don't wish to be too hard on Mr. Adams, since most of us talk this way about words every now and then. Admittedly, too, much that has been said or written about individual words has had the effect of making others use them more carefully and effectively in contexts. Perhaps it is just as easy to think and talk about words out of contexts as it is hard to use them that way. And not everyone who thinks or talks about them has the tastes in poetry that seem to be implied.

Nevertheless, there is a connection between this attitude toward words and the always popular theory that poetry ought to be written with words that are in themselves "poetic"—that it ought to draw upon a special "poetic" vocabulary and should be guided by certain established pleasant combinations of these words. Such poetry is, of course, relatively easy to read and appreciate; as a matter of fact, the reader is predisposed to have a poetic reaction to it, since it draws upon a vocabulary that has a long association with poetic contexts. Consequently, good poetry becomes identified with poetry that places no great strain on the reader: does not shock him with unseemly words, distract him with strange rhythms or spoil his pleasure with too many ideas.

This sounds a great deal like the classical dream of a literary language set apart, much as a precious antique is put out of reach of uncouth fingers, and it points to the "common sense" kind of anti-intellectualism that Arther Lovejoy finds in the 18th century. However, modern lovers of "poetic" poetry generally find themselves most at home with poetry written in the romantic tradition. It is such a vocabulary and the use made of it that is most often in mind when these people complain that modern poetry lacks verbal beauty. Had they read Wordsworth when he was first published, they would have objected to him in the same terms.

An important factor in this establishing of certain words as in themselves poetic is the instinctive tendency, observable in individuals or periods, to "fix" permanently at least the literary part of the language, so that what is conceived to be poetic can continue to be written. This tendency is in part the expression of a natural fear of time and change, and is one reason why we clutch the dictionary as convulsively as we do—as if it were the only thing that stood between us and semantic chaos.

So far as this tendency is successful it both protects and restricts the range of appreciation. If nothing opposed it the result would be a completely formalized and artificial poetry, comfortably immunized from the new and the unexpected. But it is always being opposed, and periodically the opposition takes dramatic shape: a Donne, a Wordsworth, or an Eliot refuses to believe that words can be "fixed," however beautifully.

Corollary to the belief that the beauty of language can be seen in words taken singly is the conviction that the corruption of language is most apparent in the connotative abuse of words—for instance in advertising. Countless once fine words, the argument goes, have been spoiled for poets because the ad-man has inflated them hopelessly out of shape or impregnated them with the garlic of huckstering.

The fear is exaggerated. With this statement, though, I intend no comfort to Madison Avenue, which even in its systolic phase of the soft sell, is no less semantically responsible than it was before. No doubt advertising has had its effect on language, and has so appropriated certain words that temporarily at least some writers tend to avoid them; and surely anyone concerned about language ought to resist this and all such corruptive forces. But if you will check through any anthology of modern poetry (for instance Rinehart's splendid *Fifteen Modern American Poets*) you will see how many of the presumably corrupted words are just as poetically usable as ever.

The paradox, then, is that good poetry is not made out of beautiful words: out of beautiful words you make bad poetry and perfume ads. Yet the effect of good poetry is to make words beautiful by associating them with the beauty of their contexts. The magic then seems to be a permanent property of the words themselves, ensuring poetic effects to subsequent users. A real poet knows this is not true. The better other poets write, the harder it will be for him. There are no magic, ready-made words. He must, as Eliot puts it in *Four Quartets,* begin all over again his "raid on the inarticulate / With shabby equipment always deteriorating."

DISCUSSION

Examine Mr. Sisk's sentence, "Mr. Adams' speculations, I suggest, are founded on questionable assumptions that are shared by a great number of people who also believe that they love words and literature." What does this statement imply? Does it tell you anything about Professor Sisk? What is the connotation of the statement as distinct from its denotation? What does the author mean by "a dictionary approach to language?" Consider Sisk's phrase, "systolic phrase"; do you understand what he means?

How much of Sisk's article is an attack on Adams? Can you Does he use any "hideous words"?
see any evidence of a personality clash? How objective is Sisk?

More on Ugly Words

J. DONALD ADAMS

Some time ago in this column I amused myself by discussing hideous words. Now, in an article published in *America* for February 9, I find myself taken rather solemnly to task for having ventured to suggest that the ugliness or beauty of a word counts for much, outside the context in which it is placed. Prof. John P. Sisk of Gonzaga University in Spokane, Wash., thinks that my speculations were "founded on questionable assumptions that are shared by a great number of people who also believe that they love words and literature. . . . One of these assumptions is that the beauty or hideousness of a word can be found in the word itself, isolated or abstracted from any context. This is a dictionary approach to language."

Professor Sisk says he doesn't wish to be too hard on me, "since most of us talk this way about words every now and then." If we do, I think it is with more justification than he is willing to allow. Far be it from me to quarrel with Professor Sisk when he remarks that "all communication is done with words in contexts," or that "the beauty in organized language is not so much the result of putting beautiful words together as it is in putting words together beautifully." But I disagree strongly when he adds that "it is irrelevant to ask whether words so organized are beautiful when taken singly." Certainly the whole is greater than the sum of its parts, but the parts are in themselves of great importance. Each is capable of contributing to or detracting from the total effect.

Let me use a simple illustration—one which I used once before in a discussion of beautiful words. In the Twenty-third Psalm, which I am sure Professor Sisk would grant as an instance of words which were put beautifully together, we come to the sentence, "He leadeth me beside the still waters." If you substitute "quiet" for "still," I submit that the loveliness of the phrase is seriously impaired. Not merely because the use of "quiet" makes for a less harmonious combination of sounds, but also because to my ear, at least, "still" is the more suggestive word. The liquid quality of the "l's" with which the word ends reinforces the meaning, while the sharpness of "quiet" takes something away. Is it irrelevant to pause for choice between the two words?

And does it not follow, then, that the effect of a word upon the ear—pleasing or otherwise—cannot be confined, as Professor Sisk would have it, to "playing parlor games with words as words," and that the beauty resident in a word's sound is not, as he contends it is, "useless when applied to words in context"?

Because I contend that many words do have a character of their own, independent of context, Professor Sisk concludes I must assume that unattractive sounding words are to be avoided, and proceeds to link my belief in their individual character with "the always popular theory that poetry ought to be written with words that are in themselves 'poetic'—that it ought to draw upon a special 'poetic' vocabulary and should always be guided by certain established pleasant combinations of words."

These two attitudes—belief in the individual character of words and belief in a "poetic" vocabulary—do not necessarily join. Certainly I do not subscribe to the latter, much as I believe in the first. Professor Sisk in the course of his article refers to Coleridge as "a hard man to take a stand against." Surely, then, he will allow me to quote the definitions of good prose and poetry offered by Coleridge: the one, "proper words in their proper places"; the other, "the most proper words in their proper places." I do not repeat them because, good as they are, I think they are completely satisfying, but because they throw a little light on the matters under discussion. Certainly, in the words I quoted from the Twenty-third Psalm, "quiet" would be a proper word in the proper place; "still" the most proper word in its proper place.

Professor Sisk expresses scepticism about the power of a word to evoke pleasant or beautiful sensations. "Granted," he says, "that the isolated word (provided that isolation is possible) may evoke some kind of sensation, still the sensation, or images, that concern us primarily are those evoked by words in patterns. If you test isolated words according to their power to evoke pleasant sensations, you are not only likely to be hopelessly subjective, but you will find out little about their real evocative potential." But the fact that the sensation produced by a word may be subjective in origin does not alter the potentiality of its impact. Why must the sensations or images evoked by words in a pattern be those that concern us primarily? And cannot our reaction to words in a pattern be fully as subjective as our reactions to a single, isolated word?

To anyone who doubts the possession of character by individual words, or the power resident in them, issuing from themselves, I would recommend an evening's browsing in Ivor Brown's series of word anthologies. True, we have eventually and unavoidably to deal with words in their contexts, but there is much to be gained by consideration of them by and for themselves.

DISCUSSION

"At times Adams and Sisk seem to be talking about two different things and not really listening to one another at all." Is this remark justified? How does Adams seem to react to Sisk's criticism? Can you see a difference in tone or attitude between Adams' first and second articles?

Who wins the argument? Examine and state the grounds for your decision. Who is the more objective? Cite evidence.

2

On the Background of Your Language

THE FOLLOWING SELECTIONS have to do with the history of your language. It is a very large subject; the selections can scarcely scratch the surface, but they should serve to remind you that you have inherited a very rich language. The author of the first selection, Professor Charlton Laird, teaches at the University of Nevada and is the author of many books on language in addition to several novels. The selection is from his *The Miracle of Language*. The second selection is from *A History of the English Language* by the late Professor Albert C. Baugh, an outstanding American language scholar.

English: His Sisters, His Cousins, His Aunts

CHARLTON LAIRD

We have already observed that the somewhat barbaric farmers who came to the island of Britain in the fifth and sixth centuries were a mixture of West Germanic-speaking lowlanders, mostly Angles and Saxons. Strictly speaking their language was not Anglo-Saxon and no such language existed; there were only Anglian dialects, and other Germanic dialects, which have descended with variations until this day. But Anglo-Saxon is a convenient term; not everybody knows what it means, but nobody confuses it with anything else, as they do its synonym, *Old English*. "Oh, I just love those Old English novels," an acquaintance of mine gushed, in speaking of Thomas Hardy. At least, nobody thinks Thomas Hardy wrote Anglo-Saxon. Roughly, then, the Hengist and Horsa of the Venerable Bede and all their rude pirate friends spoke what we may call Anglo-Saxon.

They continued to speak it for some hundreds of years, disturbed by nothing more than a few obstreperous Celts and one another's battle-axes. It took them a century or so to drive out or to pacify the Celts. Some of these Celts died in battle; others took sanctuary on convenient islands, Ireland and the Isle of Man, for instance. Some fled to the continent and founded a colony in what is now Brittany—named, presumably, from the British immigrants. But probably most of them stayed on the island of Britain. Those who could not live with the Germans fled to the mountains of Scotland and Wales where the invaders were not disposed to follow. The invaders were farmers, and wooded mountains are not good farming country; besides, it is often unhealthy to go among mountains if somebody on top of the mountain does not like you.

Many Celts stayed where they were, reduced to subsidiary or servile positions under the invaders. Apparently the Germans were not shockingly hard on them, provided they would surrender anything the Germans wanted, especially the best farming land. The Celtic graveyards of the period are in villages up on the hill-tops, connected by the ancient Celtic trackways. Down in the rich valleys are the Germanic graveyards. In defense of the invaders one should add, perhaps, that the Celts had not bothered with that land; it was covered with oak trees, which were hard to get rid of, and the Celts had not taken much to farming anyhow. But whether they were treated badly or not, the Celts did not love their fellow Indo-Europeans. In fact they seem to have hated them so much that although the Celts had become Roman Christians they took no chances of seeing any Germans in the Christian heaven. They declined to convert them to Christianity, thereby dooming them expeditiously to hell.

So the invading Germans fought a slow war of conquest with the native Celts, and continued fighting small dynastic wars among themselves after they had subdued the natives. They settled down and became natives themselves, and soon an ancestor of the English language was the native speech. In all this, they absorbed almost no Celtic language, as they absorbed no Celtic religion. Many Celtic names for places survive, mostly old Celtic roots with Latin endings, now changed beyond all ready recognition; for instance, *Eboracum* became *York*, and *Caer Luguvalium* became *Carlisle*. But you can search for hours through a dictionary without finding any other sort of word which the Anglo-Saxons in the valleys got from the Celts on the hilltops or the Celtic servants in the kitchen. A few Celtic words we have. A few words for place names have become common nouns, *down* for *hill*, for instance. Later, we acquired Celtic words with Celtic goods. We borrowed Celtic *whisky*, and corrupted the Celtic word for it, *usquebaugh* (water of life), but all that happened long after. The early Celts had no whisky to lend. The explanation for the meager Celtic influence upon English supposedly is that the invaders conquered slowly, keeping their own ranks intact, taking new land only when they needed it; hence there were never a few conquering Germans surrounded by large numbers of native Celts. The Celts who stayed had to learn Anglo-Saxon; the Germans never bothered to learn Celtic. The experience of the white people in what became the United States is somewhat analogous; since on the whole the whites drove the Indians before them, and kept the Indians in a servile position and few in number when the two peoples mixed, relatively few Indian words except place names have found their way into standard English. Many of our Indian words date from the day when a small number of white trappers or traders lived in a predominantly Indian culture. That seemingly did not happen in Britain; any German who found himself in a predominantly Celtic culture did not live long.

Thus the Angles and the Saxons, their friends and their dialects, became established in England. Christianity eventually found its way to them in spite of the native Celts, partly from Ireland and partly from the Continent. Several relatively large political areas, or kingdoms, took something like shape on the island. To the north and east were Northumbria and Mercia, mainly Anglian areas; to the south and west were various divisions of Saxons; at the extreme southeast tip were the descendants of the Jutes—whoever they were. They were apparently the first comers among the Germanic people. The Venerable Bede, with a handy etymological guess, said they came from Jutland, but we now know they did not. The best guess seems to be that they were professional soldiers—that is, professional international robbers; anyhow, their descendants lived mostly in what is now Kent. This was the situation when some strong-minded relatives of the Germanic invaders came to visit. They announced their arrival by sacking the Abbey of Lindisfarne late in the eighth century, and not until about the year 900 did the Anglo-Saxons have reason to hope they had stopped coming.

These guests were ... Vikings. ... They came mainly from Norway and Denmark, and they brought with them techniques which the intrepid northern sailors had worked out. They possessed long, open boats, pushed by crude sails or manned with long oars. If the oarsmen were hardy enough, these boats could be taken across the Atlantic Ocean. And they were, for the oarsmen were hardy. The combination of boats and boatmen constituted the best navy of Europe. It constituted, also, a threat to the very existence of the civilization of western Europe, for once again offense had advanced faster than defense, and civilization appeared helpless before the onslaughts of the Nordic seafarers.

The habitable parts of the island of Britain—the outlying areas harbored only wolves, Welshmen, and Scotsmen, who did not count—were divided along a line running roughly from modern London to modern Liverpool, which just happened to be about the line between the Anglian-speaking and the Saxon-speaking groups. The area to the northeast of this line became Danelaw, the country in which the law of the Danes was the law of the land, the country in which the Vikings could do as they pleased; the area to the southwest remained Saxon.

This line is the line of cleavage of British dialects until this day. To the south and west are forms descending from the Saxon dialects. To the north and east the forms descended from Anglian, as these have been altered, corrupted, and augmented with influence from Old Norse. Most medieval works composed in the north can be recognized at once, not only by grammatical differences, but also by the Norse words in the vocabulary. Many of these words have been lost in modern English or are preserved only in certain dialects not now considered standard English, which has descended mainly from the dialect of London (*bushy* in southern England can be *bosky* in the north), but to see how Viking influence upon vocabulary has persisted, one has only to look at a map of Britain. In Anglo-Saxon a common word for an inhabited place was *tun*, which in Modern English can appear as *town, ton, don, dun,* and the like. A corresponding word in Old Norse is *ham.* A glance at the map will show that southern and western areas are seeded with *Wimbledon, Brighton, Taunton, Swindon.* In the occasional occurrences of *ham* in the south, as in *Hampton, Southampton, ham* is presumably the Anglo-Saxon word for *home,* or a similar word meaning "meadow" or "river land," which did not come from Old Norse. To the north are *Nottingham, Birmingham, Durham,* and *Bullingham,* and in a truly Danish area, *North Ham, South Ham,* and *West Ham* surround *Ham.*

In this manner the Vikings left a lasting imprint upon the language of Britain, partly because so many of them stayed, and stayed clustered in their own little groups, partly because they were so important—after all, King Canute was King of Denmark before he was King of England—and partly because the languages of the invaders and the invaded were so familiar that subsequent inhabitants of Britain did not always know whether they were talking North Germanic Old Norse or West Germanic Anglo-Saxon. Nor do we always know. . . . When Robert Mannyng of Brunne wrote:

> "He toke the gate and went thru the gate"

he means to say that a man walked along the path (Old Norse *gata*) and went through the gate (Anglo-Saxon *gæt*). . . . Often we do not know whether we are speaking Old Norse or not.

DISCUSSION

Although concerned with a subject requiring a high degree of scholarship and a considerable amount of "scientific guessing," Professor Laird uses very few terms not to be found in our everyday vocabulary. Does the selection seem simplified? Do you feel you are being "talked down to"? What is the effect of Dr. Laird's candor in admitting ignorance, as when he mentions the Jutes and adds, "whoever they were"? Does his admission weaken his presentation?

For what kind of audience do you think Dr. Laird was writing? What clues can you find to lead to your conclusion? Does the author tell you anything that has any connection with your language? He is dealing with history; how does his approach differ from the kind of history you are most familiar with? Does his approach have any advantages?

The Enrichment of the Language During the Renaissance

ALBERT C. BAUGH

REJECTED WORDS.   There are some things about language that we cannot explain. One of them is why certain words survive while others do not. Among the many new words that were introduced into English ... there was a goodly number that we have not permanently retained. Some are found used a few times and then forgotten. Others enjoyed a rather longer life without becoming in any sense popular. A few were in sufficiently common use for a while to seem assured of a permanent place, but later, for some reason, lost favor and dropped out of use. *Uncounsellable,* for example, was very common in the seventeenth century, but after that practically disappeared. Some of the new words were apparently too learned and smelled too much of the lamp. *Anacephalize,* a Greek word meaning "to sum up," was of this sort and the more unnecessary since we had already adopted the Latin *recapitulate.* ... Some words might logically have survived but did not. *Expede* ~~escalated~~ (to accomplish, expedite) would have been parallel to *impede.* *Cohibit* (to restrain) is like *inhibit* and *prohibit. Demit* (to send away) was common in the sixteenth and seventeenth centuries and would have been as natural as *commit* or *transmit,* but *dismiss* gradually replaced it.... The most convincing reason for the failure of a new word to take hold is that it was not needed. *Aspectable* (visible), *assate* (to roast) and the noun *assation, exolete* (faded), *suppeditate* (furnish, supply), and many other

19

rejected words were unnecessary, and there was certainly no need for *temulent* when we had *drunk, intoxicated,* and a score of other expressions of various degrees of respectability to express the idea. ...In Shakespeare's day no one could have told whether we should say *effectual, effectuous, effectful, effectuating,* or *effective.* Two of these five options have survived. It was necessary for time to do the sifting.

WORDS FROM THE ROMANCE LANGUAGES.   Sixteenth-century purists objected to three classes of strange words, which they character-ized as *inkhorn terms, oversea language,* and *Chaucerisms.*... The English vocabulary at this time shows words adopted from more than fifty languages, the most important of which (besides Latin and Greek) were French, Italian, and Spanish. English travel in France and consumption of French books is reflected in such words as *alloy, ambuscade, baluster, bigot, bizarre, bombast, chocolate, comrade, detail, duel, entrance, equip, equipage, essay, explore, genteel, mustache, naturalize, probability, progress, re-trenchment, shock, surpass, talisman, ticket, tomato, vogue,* and *volunteer.* But the English also traveled frequently in Italy, ob-served Italian architecture and brought back not only Italian man-ners and styles of dress but Italian words. Protests against the Italianate Englishman are frequent in Elizabethan literature, and the objection is not only that the Englishmen came back corrupted in morals and affecting outlandish fashions, but that they "pow-dered their talk with oversea language." Nevertheless, Italian words like Italian fashions were frequently adopted in England. Words like *argosy, algebra, balcony, cameo, capricio* (the common form of *caprice* until after the Restoration), *cupola, design, granite, grotto, piazza, portico, stanza, stucco, trill, violin, volcano* began to be heard on the lips of Englishmen or to be found in English books. Many other Italian words were introduced through French or adapted to French forms, words like *battalion, bank-rupt, bastion, brusque, brigade, carat, cavalcade, charlatan, frigate, gala, gazette, grotesque, infantry, parakeet,* and *rebuff.* From Spanish and Portuguese English adopted *alligator (el lagarto,* the lizard) ... *maize, mosquito, mulatto, negro, pecca-dillo, potato, renegade, rusk, sarsaparilla, sombrero, tobacco,* and *yam. . . .* Thus the cosmopolitan tendency, the spirit of exploration and adventure, and the interest in the New World which was being opened up show themselves in an interesting way in the growth of our vocabulary, and contributed along with the more intellectual forms of activity to the enrichment of the English language.

THE METHOD OF INTRODUCING THE NEW WORDS. The Latin words which form so important an element in the English vocabulary have generally entered the language through the medium of writing. Unlike the Scandinavian influence and to a large extent the French influence after the Norman Conquest, the various Latin influences, except the earliest, have been the work of church-men and scholars. If the words themselves have not always been learned words, they have needed the help of learned men to become known. This was particularly true in the Renaissance. Even the words borrowed from the Romance languages in this period came in often through books, and the revivals and new formations from native material were due to the efforts of individual writers and their associates. It is impossible, of course, to say who was responsible for the introduction of each particular word, but in certain cases we can see an individual man at work—like Sir Thomas Elyot—conscious of his innovations and sometimes pausing to remark upon them. Another writer who introduced a large number of new words was Elyot's older contemporary, Sir Thomas More. To More we owe the words *absurdity, acceptance, anticipate, combustible, compatible, comprehensible, concomitance, congratulatory, . . .* and others. Elyot, besides using some of these, gives us *accommodate, adumbrate, analogy, animate, applicate, beneficence, encyclopedia, excerpt, . . .* etc. . . . So far as we now know, these words had not been used in English previously. In addition both writers employ many words which are recorded from only a few years before. And so they either introduced or helped to establish many new words in the language. What More and Elyot were doing was being done by numerous others, and it is necessary to recognize the importance of individuals as "makers of English" in the sixteenth and early seventeenth century.

ENRICHMENT FROM NATIVE SOURCES.   By far the greater part of the additions to the English vocabulary in the period of the Renaissance was drawn from sources outside of English. The popular favor shown to all kinds of foreign words seems to have implied a disparagement of English resources that was resented in some quarters. . . . Cheke so strongly opposed the borrowing of Latin and Greek words that he sought wherever possible to use English equivalents. Thus, in his translation of the Gospel of St. Matthew, where the Authorized Version reads *lunatic* he wrote *mooned,* and in the same way he said *toller* for *publican, hundreder* for *centurion, foresayer* for *prophet, byword* for *parable, freshman* for *proselyte, crossed* for *crucified, gainrising* for *resurrection.* The poets, of course, were rather more given to the revival of old words, especially words that were familiar to them in Chaucer. For this reason their revivals and new formations that suggested an older period of English were sometimes referred to as Chaucerisms.

DISCUSSION

Professor Baugh is writing about a period of great change in the language; are any of the influences and methods he mentions still at work? Can you cite any examples? What great source of new words do we have today that was practically nonexistent in the time Baugh writes about? Would it be as easy for an Elyot or a More to introduce new words today as it was in their own time? What forces are at work to stabilize English today that were not at work when Elyot and More lived? What about the effects of motion pictures, television and radio, dictionaries, and advertising?

The great increase in international travel in recent years is in some ways similar to the travel of Englishmen on the Continent that Baugh remarks on. Does modern travel affect modern English?

3

Vocabulary

IN CHAPTER 1 were selections about words and
some of the effects of words, Mr. Adams, for
example, arguing that some words are ugly and
Mr. Sisk replying that words cannot be ugly in
themselves but only as they are used. Adams
and Sisk were talking about the emotional effects of words. The following selections are
concerned with what words apparently literally
mean, what the words stand for, what we expect
to learn when we go to a dictionary and look
them up. At times the writers seem to be having
fun, just playing around with words; can you
see any serious purpose in what the writers do
in these selections?

Morning Exercises

ROBERT M. COATES

I woke up a few days ago to find myself faced with the urgent
necessity of discovering who Luke, of the term "lukewarm," was,
and why he was important enough to have a range of temperatures
named after him. I found out later, of course, as soon as I could get
to a source book—in this case, the Reverend Walter W. Skeat's
invaluable "Concise Etymological Dictionary of the English Language." "Luke" comes not from "Lucius" but from the Middle
English "luke" or "leuk," meaning "tepid," and so the addition of
"warm" seems to me a redundancy. Long before that, though,
while still abed and in the drowsy moments of half waking, I had
involved myself in a sort of offhand, random summary of all the
other shadowy, mysterious individuals who figure in our metaphorical folklore—or, at least, as many of them as I could think of
at the time.

For example, the adored and also much worried-about Pete, of
"For the love of Pete" and the anxious "For Pete's sake, don't do
that!" *What* Pete? And what would happen to him if one went
ahead and did it anyway? Or Adam. Who is he, that no one can
tell anyone else from him? Or Riley, of the luxurious life? Shank
(I see him as a farmer, somehow—a Yorkshireman, possibly—tall
and taciturn, though he also has something of Thomas Hardy in
him), of the mare? And Charley Horse; I've an equally clear picture of him. He's an Indian: fat, round-faced, greasy-skinned, and
slovenly—treacherous, too—who in the old days out West used to
hang around the trading post cadging, stealing when he could,
and spying. I'm not sure he didn't lead a raid there, killing,

Reprinted by permission; © 1960 The New Yorker Magazine, Inc.

scalping, and burning. Or was he one of the Indian chiefs who fought Custer ... ?

Ordinarily, such problems can keep me in bed for hours, not really awake but only partly so, and safely out of mischief. I don't actually make them up, either. I read somewhere recently that just as a real event—a bell, the sound of a horn in the street—can become the subject of a dream, so we all, in a sense, tend to transport our dreams into partial reality, the muscles tensing, invisibly but somehow measurably, to simulate whatever bodily activity is going on in the dream, the eyes moving, even under the closed eyelids, to follow a passing dream figure. Though I confess I can't trace any direct connection, I felt a relation somewhere between this and my own experience, for, as I say, I don't invent these little problems, enigmas, or charades; they are simply *there,* waiting for me somewhere on the dim borderland of sleep.

For the most part, I welcome them. I remember waking once, some years ago, muttering " 'A' as in 'Aye,' " and realized that at some time in the course of the night my boredom with the parrot-like " 'A' as in 'Arthur,' 'B' as in 'Boston' " code the telephone operators then used for spelling out words had asserted itself and I was at work making up a new one.

Mine, though, was to be self-defeating, designed only to cause confusion, and I worked at it busily for some time. I never did manage to get up a complete list covering the whole alphabet, but I concocted a few examples that appealed to me. " 'A' as in 'Aye,' " of course, could be varied with " 'A' as in 'Are.' " " 'E' as in 'Eye' " came next, while " 'S' as in 'See' " led to " 'C' as in 'Cue,' " and that again to " 'Q' as in 'Quai,' " which I thought was a particularly nice one. " 'Y' as in 'You' " also suggested itself, along with " 'K' as in 'Knew,' " " 'G' as in 'Gnu,' " " 'W' as in 'Wring,' " " 'H' as in 'Hour.' " There must be others. But I guess that's enough to give the general idea. Can you imagine what would happen if you tried to spell out "Schenectady"?

I suppose that because I'm a writer, the majority of my morning exercises have to do with words, and I realize that the sensible thing would be to have a shelf of reference books at my bedside so I wouldn't be forced, eventually, to get up and go prowling through the ones in my study. In that case, though, I might never

get up, and anyway many of the little muddlements that confront
me in the morning are not susceptible to that kind of research.

I woke one day recently with this question waiting for me:
"Shouldn't 'remove' mean 'move again'?" *There's* an example of
how words can turn against a person in the early hours. At the
moment, with "remake," "refill," "redouble," "recharge," and "re-
purchase" crowding into my mind, the question seemed logical; it
wasn't till the late afternoon that it occurred to me that "restore"
doesn't mean store again, either, or "request" imply another
knightly adventure.

Or again: "Respite," "despite"—why don't they rhyme? What
has the rambling "errant" to do with the purposeful "errand"? Or
the hesitant "venture" with the bold "adventure"? At such times, a
word can simply loom, like a totem devoid of meaning, in the path
toward full awakening. What is a warlock, anyway? Everyone, including Skeat, says it means a wizard, and derives from the Anglo-
Saxon *"wær"* ("truth") and *"loga"* ("liar"), or a "liar against the
truth," but I don't believe a word of it. For one thing, in Anglo-
Saxon days they *believed* in wizards; a wizard was one who divined the truth. So how could he be considered a deceiver? To
me, it's an Apache medicine man with his warlock, or scalp lock
(der. M.E. *scalp,* Icel. *scālpr,* M. Swed. *skalp*—a sheath; and
Dan. *lok,* cf. Icel. *lykkr*—a loop), dressed flauntingly for battle.
The process by which the name for the mere tuft of hair came to
represent its wearer is one familiar to all of us etymologists:
synecdoche, or the substitution of an attribute for the name of
the thing or person himself. It's as simple as that.

"Comeuppance"? "Akimbo"? The latter, according to Skeat,
comes from another witches' brew, or warlock stew, of Icel.,
Scand., and M.E. words meaning roughly "in a bent position," but
you can't believe everything Skeat says. Dedicated scholar though
he was, I suspect he was not above stretching the facts a little to
make a point, and in this case his own conscience may have
bothered him, for at the end of the passage he adds, in paren-
theses, "Very doubtful; a guess." Webster, though, takes his derivation with fewer reservations, introducing only a mild "possibly"
in the etymology—which just goes to show that it's probably
better to stay away from the reference books and do your own
interpreting in the morning.

Lately, I've been engaged in a more ambitious undertaking; namely, the rounding up of what I call the "irreducible plurals" in the language. That is, the words that, in customary usage, at least, appear in plural form only. It began, I clearly recall, with the word "oodles"—again in the early morning. "If a rich man can be said to have oodles of money" (I had waked to find the question already phrased and waiting for me), "why can't an ordinary man like myself have an oodle?" He can't, of course, and neither can he have a scad or—in respect to finance, at least—a lashing of money. "Slather," too, is out. Such things just don't come singly, and I've discovered, simply by staying comfortably abed and pondering the matter, that there are a number of other things that fall into the same category.

It is understandable, I think, that there is no such thing as a screaming meemie, a heebie-jeebie, or a solitary jitter. It's a familiar attribute of advanced stages of drunkenness—especially if a high jink or two, or a monkeyshine, has been a part of the festivity—that the subject is likely to see double, as the saying goes, and so the description of his reactions will tend toward the multiple. Naturally, then, he will wind up not a half sea, or even a whole sea, but half-seas over.

In other cases, a kind of metaphysical attitude is involved. You drop a plate on the floor and it shatters into a hundred fragments. It shatters, in short, into smithereens. If you look at the mess as a whole, it's definable: smithereens. But if you consider a single fragment, it vanishes, dialectically. There is no such thing as a smithereen—or a flinder, either, if you try to find an out that way.

There is no isolated shenanigan, I might add—and who has ever had a mump, or a measle? Altogether, there must be quite a compilation of such pluralistic oddities, and I'm sure I've by no means exhausted it. In my list of mythical personages, incidentally, I left out Jim Dandy, who, of course, is always referred to as "his nibs," wears the best of togs, and is usually dressed up to the nines. (No one, I've noticed, is ever at six and seven.) Jim also, unquestionably, lives in the smartest of digs, and I've often wondered how he would feel if he found himself in only one dig.

"Twinkletoes" is matched by "butterfingers." "Slyboots" sneaks in here somewhere, too, and so does "fiddlesticks," the most mysterious of all; conceivably one might want an extra string to the bow, but an extra bow . . . ? But haven't we had enough of such "goings on"?

I think so.

DISCUSSION

Some of the things Coates mentions have probably already occurred to you. He introduces us to etymology and his first paragraph is a good illustration of how careful reading can often lead us to the meaning of a new word without our going to the dictionary (although it is always a good idea to consult the dictionary, if only to check on our deductions). In this instance Mr. Coates wants to find out something about a word, the word "lukewarm." He is especially curious about what seems to him to be the name "Luke." Here he is engaging in what is termed folk etymology, etymology based upon apparent connections and relationships and histories that have not been checked. Coates is not here concerned with spelling or pronunciation or definition; he is curious about the history, the ancestry of the word, and he consequently goes to Skeat's *Etymological Dictionary,* where he discovers his error and incidentally the dangers of folk etymology.

In his seventh paragraph Coates applies logic to the prefix "re," asking why it apparently differs in its meaning. Look up the prefix; look up "recover" and "re-cover." Farther along Coates talks about idiomatic expressions; perhaps you can add some, like "dire straits"; can one be in just "straits"? And what about "durance vile"?

In his first paragraph Coates relates his experience in finding out where a word came from; try it yourself, using the following suggestions:

> "Mike" as in "For the love of Mike"
> "Thomas" the doubting kind
> "George" as in "Let George do it"
> "Jake" as in "Everything's Jake"
> "George" as in "By George!"
> "Buster" as in "Look here, Buster!"
> "jerry" as in "jerry-built"

Concoct some folk etymology for the word you choose; then check the etymology.

English Is a Queer Language

ALICE HAMILTON, M.D.

To realize how queer it is, one must follow the struggles of an intellectual foreigner trying to learn English. That has been our experience since Bohus Petrzelka, a doctor of laws from Prague, with his wife and little daughter, took up his abode in the roomy ell of our house. Both Petrzelka and his wife knew German well (and hated it), but during the six years of the German occupation English was forbidden, and they forgot what they had learned in school and had to start from scratch. While little Jane lapped it up as a kitten laps milk, her parents struggled along, trying to reason out the why of many strange usages which we had never realized were strange. We tried to explain, but we found it surprisingly difficult.

Jarmila came to me with this puzzle. "Mrs. Green told me her mother is coming to visit her, and she is going to stay a week. How can she stay if she is going? How can she go if she is staying?" I could not explain, because never before had I realized that "going" may have nothing to do with the verb "to go," though the latter has its own present participle which seems identical. This other "going" deals only with the future; I am going to see this matter through; he is going to lose his job; she is going to be tired out. None of these examples have anything to do with "to go." All I could say was a helpless, "Well, it is idiomatic."

The next was also a surprise and also beyond my capacity to explain. Jarmila said, "Somebody asked me if I would not miss Miss Clara while she is away. I know what it means when you say you miss the bus, but how can I miss her when she is not here?"

The next problem was much worse. Jarmila said, "Is it true that it means the same thing if you say, 'The house burned down' or 'The house burned up'? Surely if it burned up, that means the fire started in the cellar and worked up, while if it burned down, it started in the attic and worked down."

"No," I said, "it does not. You can say it either way and it means the same thing."

Jarmila sighed. "I do not understand this 'up.' I thought I knew the difference between up and down, but they tell me it is the same if I slow up my car or slow it down. And there are so many 'up's' that seem quite unnecessary. Why do they tell me to hurry up when I am not going upstairs? And why must I clean up the mess, wrap up the parcel, tidy up my desk? What has 'up' to do with it all?"

"Well," I began, rather helplessly, "perhaps 'clean up' seems more thorough than just 'clean.' "

Jarmila looked skeptical, and after a period of meditation she came back in triumph. "No," she said. " 'Up' has nothing to do with thoroughness. Look now. There are four ways you can use 'make up.' I make up the bed. I make up my mind. I make up my face when I put on rouge and lipstick. And Jane makes up with Anne when they have quarreled."

"Yes," I said, "and there is a fifth. I make up a story to entertain Jane."

Of course there was no explanation I could give her, and it sent me and the rest of the family on a search for the unnecessary "up's" we use all the time. You can put yourself to sleep chasing them down the alphabet from "add up" to "wake up," and you will find queer things, such as "up to now" and "it's up to you" and two "look up's," one meaning to raise one's eyes, the other to seek information from the encyclopedia. I gave up trying to explain "up."

What about "must"? There too the problem was quite new to me. Jarmila said, "Does not 'must' carry the meaning of compulsion or command, from oneself or somebody else? But the other day I was telling some of the neighbors how long it took me to drive to Hammonnassett Beach, and one of them said, 'You must have lost your way,' and then another said, 'You must have been pretty tired by the time you reached home.' Now nobody commanded me to lose my way or to get tired. So why 'must'?"

The next problem was a tough one. Bohus came back from work (a Czech doctor of laws cannot practice law in this country because his study has been based on Napoleonic law) saying that a man had told him that if he had learned all the ways there are in English of using the word "get" he would have mastered the language. That started us on a hunt for "get," which yielded a more abundant harvest than did Jarmila's "up."

Just try to "get" down the alphabet from "get along with somebody" to "get well." Of course we get sick, too, we get ahead of somebody, get behind in our work, get even with somebody, get homesick, get cold feet, get discharged, get rich, and so on ad infinitum. We can even, if inelegantly, "get going," and as a final triumph, we can "get our comeuppance," thus combining the two troublesome words in a very useful but quite unexplainable expression.

Jarmila and Bohus became experts at finding English words that mean three or four or more different things. Take "fall," for instance. We fall in love, we fall sick, we love the fall of the year, we fear the fall-out from the atom bomb, Christmas Day falls on a Friday. And if we are old-fashioned enough to say "it fell out," we mean "it came to pass." We keep house, we keep books, we keep silence, we keep the Sabbath day holy. We put on a hat, put off till tomorrow, put out a fire, put up with disagreeable people.

Even so simple an expression as "back and forth" arouses criticism, because it is illogical. "One can not go back if one does not first go forth. Why do you not say 'forth and back'?"

Our Czech friends tell us that the Czech language is logical and that one can explain it reasonably. English, I find, is not.

DISCUSSION

Dr. Hamilton uses the problems of her Czech guests as the means of presenting to us logical inconsistencies of our language. You may know of similar experiences which would offer more examples. The problem is one of idiom (see definition p. 174), and English is not the only language with problems of idiom; you may know a foreign language well enough to illustrate. For example, it is often noted that whereas formal usage in English requires "It is I," French requires "C'est moi (It is me)." Is

French consistent? Does it follow the same pattern of pronoun person for the third person?

Speculation about idiom can be interesting as well as informative, as Dr. Hamilton's essay shows; it might also be interesting to speculate on explanations of idiom. Can you offer any guides to idiom? What determines accepted idiomatic usage?

They Talk Past Each Other

IRVING LEE

"It takes," says Thoreau, in the noblest and most useful passage
I remember to have read in any modern author, "two to speak truth
—one to speak and another to hear."—Robert Louis Stevenson,
"Truth of Intercourse," *Virginibus Puerisque,* J. M. Dent & Sons,
1925, p.32.

HOW MISUNDERSTANDING HAPPENS. The one thing people tend to
take for granted when talking to others is that they understand
each other. It is rare, indeed, in a meeting to have someone hold
up his own argument long enough to say, "I think you said. . . . Did
you?" or "Was I right in thinking you meant . . . ?" We found
people ever so eager to parry what a man says without ever
wondering whether *that* is what the man said.

In the give-and-take of talk things go fast, and one is so busy
organizing his reply that he doesn't take the time to make sure
he knows what he is replying to. This is unfortunate because it
often means that, instead of talking with others, people talk past
or by-pass each other.

Note some by-passings.

1. The British Staff prepared a paper which they wished to raise as
a matter of urgency, and informed their American colleagues that they
wished to "table it." To the American staff "tabling" a paper meant
putting it away in a drawer and forgetting it. A long and even acrimonious argument ensued before both parties realized that they were
agreed on the merits and wanted the same thing.[1]

2. I remember a worrisome young man who, one day, came back
from the X-ray room wringing his hands and trembling with fear. "It

[1]Winston Churchill, "The Second World War," Vol. III, Book II, *The New
York Times,* February 28, 1950, p. 31.

is all up with me," he said. "The X-ray man said I have a hopeless cancer of the stomach." Knowing that the roentgenologist would never have said such a thing, I asked, "Just what did he say?" and the answer was on dismissing him, the roentgenologist said to an assistant, "N.P." In Mayo clinic cipher this meant "no plates," and indicated that the X-ray man was so satisfied with the normal appearance of the stomach on the X-ray screen that he did not see any use in making films. But to the patient, watching in an agony of fear for some portent of disaster, it meant "nothing possible": in other words that the situation was hopeless![2]

3.   A foreman told a machine operator he was passing: "Better clean up around here." It was ten minutes later when the foreman's assistant phoned: "Say, boss, isn't that bearing Sipert is working on due up in engineering pronto?"

"You bet your sweet life it is. Why?"

"He says you told him to drop it and sweep the place up. I thought I'd better make sure."

"Listen," the foreman flared into the phone, "get him right back on that job. It's got to be ready in twenty minutes."

. . . What [the foreman] had in mind was for Sipert to gather up the oily waste, which was a fire and accident hazard. This would not have taken more than a couple of minutes, and there would have been plenty of time to finish the bearing. Sipert, of course, should have been able to figure this out for himself—except that something in the foreman's tone of voice, or in his own mental state at the time, made him misunderstand the foreman's intent. He wasn't geared to what the foreman had said.[3]

4.   A lady recently ordered some writing paper at a department store and asked to have her initials engraved thereon. The salesgirl suggested placing them in the upper right-hand corner or the upper left-hand corner, but the customer said no, put them in the center. Well, the stationery has arrived, every sheet marked with her initials equidistant from right and left and from top and bottom.[4]

5.   In a private conversation with Mr. Molotov, it became apparent that another difficult misunderstanding in language had arisen between ourselves and the Russians. At the San Francisco Conference when the question of establishing a trusteeship system within the United Nations was being considered, the Soviet delegation had asked Mr. Stettinius

[2]Walter C. Alvarez, *Nervousness, Indigestion and Pain*, Paul B. Hoeber, Inc., 1943, p. 74.

[3]*The Foreman's Letter*, National Foreman's Institute, Inc., February 8, 1950, p. 3.

[4]"The Talk of the Town," *The New Yorker*, January 28, 1950, p. 21. Reprinted by permission. Copyright, 1950, The New Yorker Magazine, Inc.

what the American attitude would be toward the assumption by the Soviet Union of a trusteeship. Mr. Stettinius replied in general terms, expressing the opinion that the Soviet Union was "eligible" to receive a territory for administration under trusteeship. Mr. Molotov took this to mean we would support a Soviet request for a trusteeship.[5]

In each case a word or phrase or sentence was used one way by the speaker and interpreted in another way by the listener. This is possible because words are versatile. Except for those intended for highly specialized purposes (like tetrasporangium, icosahedron, bisulfite), it is not unusual to find most words put to rather varied uses. A seventh-grade class in English was able to make up thirty sentences in which the word "set" was used differently each time. Even "word" is listed in sixteen different ways in *The American College Dictionary*.

The naïve speaker of a language usually has the feeling that, in general, words have a meaning, and he is seldom conscious of the great "area" of meaning for all except highly technical words. It is in this respect that the student's observation first needs widening and sharpening. Frequently we have tried to "build vocabularies" by adding more units or words. But to push first the addition of more vocabulary units in order to increase the number of words may interfere with, rather than help, effective mastery of language. This is the process that produces a Mrs. Malaprop. Most frequently the student needs first to know well the various areas of use of the units he is already familiar with; he needs to be made conscious of the great diversity of uses or meanings for commonly used words. He must be made aware, for example, that the statement "The children did not *count*" can mean that they did not *utter the words* for the numbers in a series, or that the children *were not considered*. Ordinarily we just don't believe without considerable careful examination that for the five hundred most used words in English (according to the Thorndike *Word Book*) the Oxford Dictionary records and illustrates from our literature 14,070 separate meanings.[6]

At different times the same words may be used differently.

When Francis Bacon referred to various people in the course of his *Essays* as *indifferent, obnoxious,* and *officious,* he was describing them as "impartial," "submissive," and "ready to serve." When King James II

[5]James F. Byrnes, *Speaking Frankly,* Harper & Brothers, 1947, p. 96.
[6]Charles C. Fries, "Using the Dictionary," *Inside the ACD,* October 1948, p. 1.

observed that the new St. Paul's Cathedral was *amusing, awful,* and *artificial,* he implied that Sir Christopher Wren's recent creation was "pleasing, awe-inspiring, and skilfully achieved." When Dr. Johnson averred that Milton's *Lycidas* was *"easy, vulgar,* and therefore *disgusting,"* he intended to say that it was "effortless, popular, and therefore not in good taste."[7]

A role of experience also affects the varieties of usage. Brander Matthews provided an example from a dinner-party conversation:

> The second topic . . . was a definition of the image called up in our several minds by the word *forest.* Until that evening I had never thought of forest as clothing itself in different colors and taking on different forms in the eyes of different men; but I then discovered that even the most innocent word may don strange disguises. To Hardy forest suggested the sturdy oaks to be assaulted by the woodlanders of Wessex; and to Du Maurier it evoked the trim and tidy avenues of the national domain of France. To Black the word naturally brought to mind the low scrub of the so-called deer-forests of Scotland; and to Gosse it summoned up a view of the green-clad mountains that towered up from the Scandinavian fiords. To Howells it recalled the thick woods that in his youth fringed the rivers of Ohio; and to me there came back swiftly the memory of the wild growths bristling up unrestrained by man, in the Chippewa Reservation which I had crossed fourteen years before in my canoe trip from Lake Superior to the Mississippi. Simple as the word seemed, it was interpreted by each of us in accord with his previous personal experience.[8]

This conclusion about the range and possible uses of a word is easily verified. When it is forgotten, a listener just as easily comes to believe that (1) there is but one way to use a word—*his*—and (2) the speaker is doing with his words what the listener would were the listener doing the talking.

Can you see these beliefs at work in the examples given above?

In short, what *you* understand by any word or statement may not be what someone else intends to say. In a way, this is so ob-

[7]Simeon Potter, *Our Language,* Pelican Books, 1950, p. 116.

[8]Brander Matthews, *These Many Years: Recollections of a New Yorker,* Charles Scribner's Sons, 1917, pp. 287–288. Quoted from the essay by Allen Walker Read, "Linguistic Revision as a Requisite for the Increasing of Rigor in Scientific Method," read at the Third Congress on General Semantics, July 22, 1949.

vious that most of us feel no obligation to think more about it. However, when one is aware of the fact it does not necessarily follow that he will act in terms of it. And there is some evidence that, unless people can be made sensitive to the possibility of by-passing, they make only meager efforts to stop it.

IT TAKES TWO TO MAKE COMMUNICATION. I have no wish here to give comfort to the bore who gets so much pleasure squelching discussions with his defiant "Define your terms." His maneuver results in shifting the burden in communication to the other fellow. Both must be brought into the act. We would have the listener work just a bit, too. So we urge him to state his notion of what was being said. Incidentally, that bore may sometimes be routed with this: "What definition of my words have you in mind? Perhaps we are thinking together after all."

The "plain-talk" and "say-it-in-simple-words" teachers have been in vogue but they haven't been especially helpful. They, too, tend to put the emphasis on one side of the communication line. Putting the burden for understanding on the speaker is a kind of implied invitation to the listener to sit back and contentedly assume he has nothing to do but wait his turn. And besides, even the simple words have uses which too frequently vary between man and man.

We once observed eight meetings of a group of nine men, who functioned as a standing committee in a corporation having wide public responsibilities. Five had taken one or more courses and had studied some of the books on "talking plainly." One of the items checked had to do with "the assumption of understanding." Can men be differentiated according to their readiness to believe they know what the other fellow is referring to? We looked in their replies for such indications as *questions* for assurance that the asker is "with" the speaker, *qualifications* like "If I understand what you say" or "If I knew what you mean. . . ."*invitations* like "Correct me if I'm off the beam" or "Tell me whether I answered what you intended to say. . . ."

We were hardly prepared to find that four of the "plain-talk students" did the least amount of questioning, qualifying, inviting, etc. This may, of course, be an accident. Before a conclusion worth much can be drawn we should have a broader sampling of the population. And before a cause can be assigned with confidence much more investigation would be needed. Nevertheless, *these particular men,* knowing the ways to "plainness" and using them, tended to think they had done enough when they spoke so. They seemed to focus attention on *their* talking. They made no comparable effort to look to the character of what they heard.

I am not at all arguing that this finding in these particular cases means that training in plain talking makes for poor listening. I am trying to suggest only that training in the explicit effort at understanding may be a difficult sort of thing and may not automatically carry over from other training.

Cardinal Manning once said something relevant:

> I have no doubt that I will hear that I am talking of what I do not understand; but in my defence I think I may say, I am about to talk of what I do not understand for this reason: I cannot get those who talk about it to tell me what they mean. I know what I mean by it, but I am not at all sure that I know what they mean by it; and those who use the same words in different senses are like men that run up and down the two sides of a hedge, and so can never meet.

It is helpful to think of the radio in this. The performer in the studio can talk his heart out, but if the man in the easy chair is tuned in elsewhere it really makes no difference what is being said. Unless the receiver is on the same wave length, the character of what is sent out hardly governs the communication process.[9]

This is not to imply that a speaker cannot help by putting what he has to say in clear, listenable language. Anything he does to define, simplify, amplify, illustrate, is all to the good. But it is only part of the process. The listener has a job to do, too. He must make the effort to come to terms with the speaker to keep from assuming that he inevitably knows what the speaker has in mind. At the very least he might temper his arrogance with a question now and then just to make sure.

It takes two to make communication.

[9]This image is well developed in the article by Charles T. Estes, "Speech and Human Relations in Industry," *The Quarterly Journal of Speech,* April 1946, pp. 160–169.

ARE YOU ON HIS COMMUNICATION LINE?   The preceding pages of
this chapter were mimeographed and given to three groups, one
meeting for study of the Bible, one considering matters of policy
in a business corporation, and one working on problems in the administration of a college fraternity. Every member of each group
read a portion out loud. We then talked about the main point—it
takes two to make communication. We agreed that this was rather
simple stuff and that we would try to talk with the possibility of
by-passing in mind. We agreed, further, that no one of us would
be insulted if asked to clarify or "talk some more" on any doubtful
point. Nor would anyone feel hesitant about trying to get on the
same wave length with anyone else. We gave each a small card
with the inscription, "Are you on *his* communication line?"

What happened?

In each case the business of the meeting was slowed down. Only
half as many items on the agenda could be covered. There was a
certain amount of unfruitful wrangling about small points. Some
members became tongue-tied in the face of so much freedom.
Others became impatient with what seemed a waste of time, this
trying to get to the speaker. The first sessions were always the
worst. Most members felt comfortable only after the second
or third.

And then we came upon something interesting. A man was
being listened to. He found that others were actually waiting
until he finished. He felt flattered in turn by the fact that another
was trying to reach him rather than argue at him. He found himself trying to make his points so that his hearers would have less
trouble with them. They were trying harder to read the cards he
was putting on the table. The ornery member, normally so quick
to doubt, stayed to question. The timid member found that the
social pressure about the participation was all on his side.

We are inclined to think that the long-run results were worth
the time and trouble.

THE PURIST'S DOGMA.   In a number of experimental discussion
groups generous enough to submit to such instruction there was
a curious resistance to this seemingly obvious doctrine. I would

be asked questions like these: Do you mean to say that a word doesn't have some definite, accurate meaning of its own regardless of the person who uses it? Isn't there a right or correct use for each word? If somebody fails to use a word exactly isn't he violating some rule in rhetoric or grammar?

How did these people come under the spell of the purist's dogma? Were they remembering some menacing drillmaster with a word list asking "what is *the* meaning of ——?" Or had they been badgered by vocabulary tests with entries like *glabrous heads: bald, over-sized, hairy, square, round; his stilted manner: irresolute, improper, cordial, stiffly formal* with instructions to circle the meaning? Or maybe they grew up when Alexander Woollcott was campaigning against certain current usage. He fought the use of "alibi" as a synonym for excuse; he wanted it saved for its "elsewhere" sense. He sneered when "flair" was used in the sense of knack or aptitude. He wanted it reserved for "capacity to detect." He and the traditional handbooks had a long list of such "reservations."

Or maybe they got their moorings from the pronouncements of Richard Grant White, who once said, "There is a misuse of words that can be justified by no authority, however great, and by no usage however general." Or maybe they got no further in *Through the Looking Glass* than

". . . How old did you say you were?"
Alice made a short calculation, and said, "Seven years and six months."
"Wrong!" Humpty Dumpty exclaimed triumphantly. "You never said a word like it!"
"I thought you meant 'How old *are* you?' " Alice explained.
"If I'd meant that, I'd have said it," said Humpty Dumpty.

Regardless of the source, they used this dogma as the basis for a theory of their own about the cause of misunderstanding. If a speaker didn't use a word correctly it was only natural if a listener who did know the exact meaning was misled. Just get people to use words in their right meaning and then everyone will understand everyone else.

Indeed, this might be a way—but how can we do it? Who has the authority to declare *the* correct use and who has the time to learn it? There are more than 600,000 words in the Merriam-Webster unabridged dictionary and perhaps half as many more in the technical vocabularies of medicine, engineering, law, etc. And when the dictionary gives several meanings, which is *the* one? And just how is anyone going to curb those who, like Humpty Dumpty, would have their own ways with words:

"... Impenetrability! That's what I say!"

"Would you tell me please," said Alice, "what that means?"

"Now you talk like a reasonable child," said Humpty Dumpty, looking very much pleased. "I meant by 'impenetrability' that we've had enough of that subject, and it would be just as well if you'd mention what you mean to do next, as I suppose you don't mean to stop here all the rest of your life."

"That's a great deal to make one word mean," Alice said in a thoughtful tone.

"When I make a word do a lot of work like that," said Humpty Dumpty, "I always pay it extra."

And what is more crucial, why do we look at words alone? Are words not most often used with other words in phrases, clauses, sentences? May not the setting affect the word?

We tried to get around this ill-advised zeal for exactness by suggesting that a word might be compared with a tool which can be used in a variety of ways. Thus, a screwdriver might be designed to drive screws, but once available it can be used to stir paint, jimmy a tight window, or, lacking any other weapon, to defend oneself with. You might, if you wish, insist that the screw function is the "right" or "correct" one and that a pistol is a much more effective weapon. But your insistence will hardly stop me from using the screwdriver in these other ways if I find it convenient or necessary to do so. A carpenter with a full rack of tools may have good reason for reserving each for but one use, but if some other purpose is served there is nothing in the nature of the tool which could prevent that other use. The desire for the restriction, then, is personal rather than functional.

Within limits, especially in technical disciplines, it is possible to standardize word usage. One is usually safe in assuming that the workers in specialized areas will conform to some established, stipulated word usages. In the military establishment and in legal affairs, for example, it is often possible as well as necessary to insist that particular words be used in particular ways.

Once outside the range of the specialist's interests, however, we are wise if we expect words to be used variously. A speaker's concern at any moment is not to use a word but to make a statement. In his eagerness to speak his piece he is more concerned with his continuous expression than with his total effect. If he happens to range outside his listeners' conventional usage, they will get nowhere lamenting his lexicographical heresy. And if they do not get to his usage they are likely to assume that he said what he never intended to.

We have come to see wisdom in this advice: Never mind what words mean. What did *he* mean?

It may take time to find out what a man means. It may demand a patient listening and questioning. It may be an unexciting effort. But it should help to bring people into an area of awareness which they are too often on the outside of. Mr. Justice Jackson's experience in a situation more momentous than anything we were exposed to adds to our confidence in the advice:

It was my experience with the Soviet lawyers at Nurnberg that the most important factor in collaboration with the Soviet was patiently and persistently to make sure, when a proposition is first advanced, that it is thoroughly understood and that both sides are using their words to express the same sense. When this was done, the Soviet lawyers kept their agreements with us quite as scrupulously as American lawyers would. They may or may not regard that as a compliment, but my intentions are good. But it was my experience that it took infinite patience with them, as they thought it took infinite patience with us, to get to a point where there was a real meeting of minds as distinguished from some textual abstract formula which both could accept only because concretely it meant nothing or meant different things to each. And I have sometimes wondered how much misunderstanding could have been avoided if arrangements between the two countries had not often been concluded so hurriedly, in the stress of events, that this time-consuming and dreary process of reducing generalities to concrete agreements was omitted.[10]

[10]Excerpt from address by Mr. Justice Robert H. Jackson at the Bar Dinner of the New York County Lawyers' Association, December 8, 1949.

DISCUSSION

Mr. Lee's title is interesting; what does he mean when he says that people "talk past each other"? Have you ever done this? Recall occasions when this has been done to you; can you make any generalizations about the kinds of occasions? Does Lee's "they talk past each other" mean about the same as the expression, "They talk at people, not with them"?

What can be said about the introductory quotation? How can it take *two* to *speak* truth? Would it not be more accurate to say it takes one to speak and another to hear truth? The key word here is, of course, *truth*.

About: New Words

MARTIN TOLCHIN

Lexicographers are perplexed daily by the problems that arise from our nation's unceasing efforts to increase its vocabulary. What is a word? At what point does it come into existence? And who is the authority for it?

Currently, dictionary men are wrestling with such terms as "exurbanite," "duopoly," "musicology," "medic," "litterbug," "hard-top," "elasticize," "desegregation," "egghead," "tranquilizer," and "paperback." Are these words? Not to mention the television meaning of "compatible" and "ghosts" and the "bop" meaning of "dig," "cool," and "crazy." Are these valid uses of established words? Finally, how might they achieve the dignity of a dictionary listing?

"A word," says Dr. Mario Pei, Professor of Romance Philology at Columbia University, "is a sound or combination of sounds taken as one unit forming a single unit of meaning." Dr. Pei estimates that the English language has increased from 100,000 words at the time of the Norman Conquest to over 1,000,000 words today —a growth which will give some idea of the amount of work necessary to keep a modern dictionary modern. And new words are being added at an unprecedented rate.

While most laymen look to the dictionary to see if a particular "combination of sounds" is actually a word, lexicographers have come around to the opposite point of view. The authority for a word—in fact, the authority for a language—they now agree rests with the users of the language. Thus the process of adding new words to the dictionary begins with a systematic examination of almost everything printed in English, including best-selling novels, regional newspapers, mail order catalogues, menus, consumer magazines, trade journals, house organs—even the labels on canned goods.

Most new words are absorbed gradually into the language, but there are exceptions. An awesome example is the phrase "atomic bomb." When it crossed the desk of a Merriam-Webster editor back in 1917 (it had been clipped from a sentence in the *Yale Review,* which read, "When you can drop just one atomic bomb and wipe out Paris or Berlin, war will have become monstrous and impossible"), it drew the penciled comment: "Fanciful." During the thirties, the phrases "atomic energy" and "atomic ray" warranted dictionary listing, but "atomic bomb" remained in the realm of the improbable. It was not until 1945 that it exploded into print, when the bomb itself was dropped on Hiroshima.

"Freeway" presents a more typical case. It first appeared in the New York *Times,* the *Saturday Evening Post, Time,* and *Harper's* during 1948–49. In these first references the word was cradled in quotes. Later the quotes were dropped and the word was bolstered by parenthetical explanations. By 1952 it was listed with the addenda of the big dictionaries and today can be found in the regular listings of recently revised works.

Once a new word is sighted (and cited), it becomes a candidate for the dictionary, and is taken up and mulled over at periodic conferences. The decision to include a word is made on the basis of its frequency and range of use. But lexicographers do not simply tally up the number of citation slips. From the citations come clues on definition, etymology, pronunciation, variant spellings, and the like.

Sometimes the file on a new word is barren. This happens with words and phrases that gain speedy acceptance. To determine the etymology of the phrase "iron curtain," for example, lexicographers wrote to Sir Winston Churchill, who had coined it. Sir Winston, it turned out, had reference to the iron curtain (since replaced by one made of asbestos) that separated the stage from the orchestra in legitimate theatres.

Practical considerations play their part in the march of a word into the boldface listings of a dictionary. Chief among these is the scope of the dictionary and the physical limitations imposed by the patching or resetting of large numbers of plates. Space for new entries is created mainly by rewriting definitions on the same page to eliminate runovers. To make space for "cybernetics," for example, the editors of the *American College Dictionary* took one line from the definition of "cyanine"; reduced the illustration of a "cycloid"; cut an example of the usage of the word "cut"; shortened the space separating the end of the "C" listings from the beginning of the "D" listings; and cut five runovers.

And Scrabble players to the contrary, there are countless bona fide words *not* listed in a dictionary, according to Jess Stein, managing editor of the *American College Dictionary*. The apparatus for gathering data on new words is far from foolproof, lexicographers agree. In addition, obscenities—"perfectly good words," Mr. Stein advises—are omitted from dictionaries because of intense competition for the home and school markets.

What of the future? "More words," predicts Mr. Stein, "because language is a mirror. It reflects what we're doing and thinking. There's no saturation point for a living language because there's no saturation point for human activities and concepts."

DISCUSSION

Do you agree with Dr. Pei's definition of a word? Is it complete enough for your purposes? According to Dr. Pei's estimate the English language has increased its number of words by ten times in about 900 years; averaged out over that period, the increase is then about 100,000 words every century, or about 1,000 words every year. Do you learn 1,000 new words every year? Awesome as that figure may be, it is totally inadequate to convey the real situation, for the vast majority of the new words have been added in modern times, and we cannot expect the loss of words to help very much, for words die slowly.

Tolchin's fourth paragraph emphasizes a point often ignored or even denied by laymen. When the everyday user of the language wants to know about a word he is likely to inquire, "What does the dictionary say?" As Tolchin points out, when the lexicographers want to know about a word, they ask, "How is it being used?" Does this mean most of us use a dictionary incorrectly? Are we, then, unable to look to a dictionary as an authority on usage?

Compile a list of words you think should be added to the next edition of the dictionary; consider how you would label them— slang, colloquial, standard. What is your opinion about the omission of obscenities? How can Mr. Stein call them "perfectly good words"?

4

The Word-Hoard

THIS SECTION begins with an essay by Mitford Mathews taken from *College Composition and Communication,* a periodical published by the National Council of Teachers of English; Mathews is addressing college English teachers. How does the audience affect the style? Mathews opens with an analogy, comparing a dictionary to a carpenter's steel square; he is attempting to get us to look upon the dictionary as a kind of tool, one which, like the square, is rarely used for more than a fraction of its potential. Perhaps he may be also attempting to dispel the common view of the .dictionary as a kind of book of rules on words, a view expressed by "What does the dictionary say?" If we follow Mathews' argument we find him telling us that the dictionary "says" nothing; instead it provides information about words, as the carpenter's square provides information about angles, which we can use to find out things about how words work.

Mortimer Adler, perhaps best known for his work in the Great Books program of the University of Chicago, seems in his essay to be learning even as the newest student; he seems genuinely interested in and even at times surprised at what he discovers in his dictionary. For example, look at his paragraph on "commerce." Are you surprised to learn that "commerce," "mercenary," and "mercy" are related?

The last five selections are argumentative. A new edition of *Webster's Third New International Dictionary of the English Language,* popularly called the *Third,* appeared in 1961. This is the dictionary most people refer to when they speak of the "unabridged"; it is the big one you commonly find in libraries. G. C. Merriam Co., the publishers, were the successors to Noah Webster, and their "big" dictionary has long been considered by many as the ultimate authority for American English. The *Third* aroused much argument, as you will see from the essays. The article by Wilson Follett, from the *Atlantic Monthly,* led the complaints; the three newspaper editorials attacked the *Third;* Bergen Evans defended it.

The Freshman and His Dictionary

MITFORD M. MATHEWS

When I was a small boy a carpenter once said in my presence that few workmen, even among master mechanics, knew more than a fraction of the uses of an ordinary steel square. The remark amazed me, as at that early age I thought a carpenter's square was a very simple tool. It certainly appeared so to me,—nothing more than two flat pieces of metal forming a right angle, and useful in marking a plank that one wished to saw in two in something like a workmanlike manner. True, the instrument has numerous markings and numbers on it, but I had never seen anyone making the slightest use of these, so I concluded they might be ignored.

When I became older and found that large books have been written on the uses of the steel square, I changed my mind about the simplicity of the tool and the limited range of its usefulness. For many years as I have observed the use made of dictionaries by even good students, I have been reminded of that remark by the carpenter about steel squares.

Dictionaries are tools, and they are much more complicated, and capable of many more uses than students suspect. All of us know students need encouragement and guidance in the use of dictionaries, and perhaps there are few teachers of freshman composition but that devote a part of their program to an effort to help students form the habit of consulting dictionaries. Composition books for freshmen point out the need for instruction of this kind.

Despite what is being done, however, the fact is easily observable that few students are able to use their dictionaries with anything like efficiency. Certainly there must be very few of those who come up through the grades these days who are not familiar with the details of looking up words in dictionaries, but it is one thing to find a word in a dictionary and quite another to understand fully the information there given about it. It seems to me that college freshmen are fully prepared for and could profit by a well-planned introduction to the larger of the English dictionaries, and an acquaintance with what they contain. Such a program might well include material of the following kinds.

1. Students should know something about the large, unabridged dictionaries to which they have ready access in college. They might well be given brief sketches of the *Oxford English Dictionary*, the *English Dialect Dictionary*, by Joseph Wright, the old *Century Dictionary* (12 volumes), and the modern unabridged *Webster*. These may be called the "Big Four" in the dictionary field, and while it is certainly not anticipated that the freshman will ever provide himself with all of them, it is a cultural experience for him to become acquainted with the circumstances under which each of them was produced, and with the special excellencies each exhibits.

An acquaintance with these larger works will not only make the student aware of what kind of information about words is available in them, but it will leave him much better prepared to make efficient use of the desk-size dictionary with which he has some familiarity.

Many years ago a graduate student inconvenienced himself greatly to come a long distance to see me to ask if I could help him secure some information about the term "poll tax." He was preparing a doctor's thesis, he told me, and needed to know how long this term had been in the language, what its basic meaning was, and what other meanings it may have had in the course of its use in English. He was most surprised when I opened the *OED* to the appropriate place and showed him that all he needed to know about this term had been available within a few feet of his desk in the school where he was studying. It is not at all likely that any but the exceptional student will ever need all the information about words that the larger dictionaries afford, but it is well worth the while of every student to become acquainted with the fact that such information is available for those who at any time need to make use of it.

It is to be hoped that in such general instruction as may be given about the different dictionaries, some emphasis will be placed on the fact that modern dictionaries do their utmost to *record* usage, not to *prescribe* it. The tendency to regard the lexicographer as a linguistic legislator is so deep-seated that it will probably never be entirely overcome. The habit of thought that is back of such expressions as "the dictionary now permits us to pronounce it thus," has been with us for a long time, and will continue. But every student should have the wholesome experience of being taught that dictionaries attempt to give commonly accepted usage, and that correctness in the use of language varies sometimes according to time and place.

2. Along with some information about the origin and scope of the large dictionaries mentioned, there should be given some elementary information about the history of the English language and the place it occupies with reference to the others of the Indo-European group. I am certainly not foolish enough to suggest that all teachers of freshman composition become instructors in Germanic philology. What I have in mind is nothing more detailed than could be easily covered in one, or at most two, class sessions, the over-all relationships of the languages being presented briefly, with a few well chosen examples to indicate the relationship of a few of them.

The desirability of this elementary acquaintance with the linguistic position occupied by English is brought out quite clearly by Professor Pei in his *Story of Language:*

Many years ago, I was requested to tutor in French a young girl who had to take College Entrance Examinations. Knowing that she had had four years of Latin as well as three years of French, I spared no occasion in the course of the tutoring to remind her that certain French words which she had difficulty in remembering came from Latin words which she knew. For a time she took it patiently, though with a somewhat bewildered air. But one day she finally blurted out: "Do you mean to tell me that there is a *connection* between Latin and French?" In the course of four years of one language and three of the other, it had never occurred to any of her Latin teachers to inform her that Latin had descendants, or to her French teacher to tell her that French had a progenitor!

208585

3. The attention usually devoted to instruction in the use of the dictionary apparently stresses spellings, meanings, and pronunciations somewhat in the order here given. Certainly these are conspicuous features of any dictionary, and it is altogether desirable for students to be encouraged to turn to these works when they are confronted with a problem of the kind indicated.

The impression, however, inevitably conveyed by instruction restricted altogether to employing the dictionary as a problem-solver, is that such a book is of no particular use unless there is a problem requiring immediate attention. Students are sorely tempted to so manipulate things as to avoid encountering problems that drive them to a dictionary. It is to be feared that, for many of them, the dictionary is a form of medicine to be resorted to only in time of unavoidable need. They associate it perhaps with castor oil or some other undesirable, dynamic type of cathartic. It is a most helpful thing for the student to learn that dictionaries are filled with interesting information from which one can derive much pleasure and instruction, even though he may not be confronted with an urgent problem of any kind.

Students should be encouraged to develop a wholesome curiosity about words that present no particular problem in spelling, pronunciation, or meaning. As a rule, the words we know well do not rise to the surface of our consciousness. It is only rarely that some common, everyday term forces itself upon our attention so urgently that for the first time we turn to the dictionary to see what lies back of it.

This use of the dictionary when there is no immediate, pressing need to do so, this giving attention to words we have known for a long time but have never grown curious about, is most rewarding. This kind of use of the dictionary we may think of as the labor of free men; the forced use is more properly likened to that of slaves.

On every hand there are words of fascinating backgrounds about which the dictionary has much to teach us. Certainly the name *Jesus,* that of the founder of Christianity, is well known to all those with whom you and I come in contact. Perhaps few of us have ever felt impelled to look the word up in a dictionary or even realized that dictionaries contain it. An examination of the dictionary, however, reveals that the name his parents gave the Saviour was Joshua, and it was by this thoroughly Jewish name that He was known by those He lived among.

The first accounts of His life were written in Greek, and in these writings *Joshua* was transliterated into *Jesus,* a name that is certainly not Jewish in its present dress and at the same time appears odd as a Greek name.

Not even a grade-school pupil is likely to be baffled by *ostrich,* but one who is allergic to words may well become curious about it. Allow it to become the focus of your attention for a moment and see how odd the word appears. Make a guess as to where you think it might have come from, and then check up on yourself by turning to the dictionary. You may be surprised, as I was, to find the word is made up of two, one from Latin and one from Greek, which have so blended as to obscure altogether the fact that the expression signifies "bird-bird" or "bird-sparrow." It is a good term to bear in mind and use upon those of our brethren who insist that only "pure English" should be used, and profess to be pained by such obvious hybrids as *cablegrams* and *electrocute.*

There may be a few teachers who have discovered how rewarding it is to look curiously at the scientific terms used in dictionaries in the definitions of plants and animals. These expressions are usually hurried over by most of us as being the exclusive property of scientists and of very little interest for others.

It is surprisingly interesting to linger over such terms. It is a gratifying experience to discover one that yields its significance somewhat readily. Our common mocking bird, for instance, is *Mimus polyglottos.* The ingenuity needed for deciphering this expression is possessed by all of us. *Mimic* and *polyglot* are all we need to see that our expression means "the many-tongued mimic," a fitting description of the bird in question.

In the spring when the snow has melted, and the earth is warming up from its long cold sleep, the cheerful piping notes of a very small frog begin to be heard in the woods and marshes. People call this little creature a *spring peeper* because of the season when his little peeping notes are first heard, but scientists dub him *Hyla crucifer.* As we puzzle over this name we are likely to give up on *Hyla* for there is no other word in the English language with

LORETTE WILMOT LIBRARY
NAZARETH COLLEGE

which we can, perhaps, associate it profitably. It has descendants among us, but we are not likely to be acquainted with them.

Crucifer though is easier. Even if we do not know that a *crucifer* is one who carries a cross, especially in a church procession, we can reason out the two elements in the word and see that it must have the meaning of one who carries a cross. Our ability to reason out this much of the scientific expression may increase our curiosity about the first element *Hyla*. Here is a helpful hint. As we all know, these scientific genus names are often from Greek. So we are reasoning sensibly when we suppose *Hyla* is Greek.

The fact is elementary that when we are confronted with a Greek word which begins with an *h*, i.e., with a rough breathing, it behooves us as cautious scouts to cast about in our minds for a possible Latin cognate beginning with an *s*. Substituting an *s* in *hyla* we come up with *syla*. Let us study *syla* a bit. It is almost a word. If we might be so bold as to insert a -v- and make it *sylva* we have a word that is in our dictionary, and one we met in a slightly different form, *silva*, when we studied first-year Latin.

The little detail of why this -v- is necessary need not bother us in the slightest at this point, because we are just having fun with no idea of becoming linguisticians. And this is it. *Hyla* and *sylva* go together and they both mean wood or forest. Now we can interpret this *Hyla crucifer* "the (little) fellow who lives in the woods and carries a cross," and when we find that this spring peeper has a dark marking on his back shaped like a cross, we are indeed gratified that now light is shining where previously all was darkness.

A teacher who is fortunate enough to have an assiduously cultivated curiosity about words will over and over again bring to a class gleanings of unexpected sorts from dictionaries. Such sharing of treasures will do more than anything else to bring home to students the fact that dictionaries are not dull, enlarged spelling books. They are filled with such a number of things that we can never exhaust their treasures but we can all be as happy as kings as we come time after time upon interesting nuggets of the kind just mentioned.

DISCUSSION

Why does Mitford Mathews begin an essay about the dictionary by discussing the carpenter's square? An analogy is a device, a way of getting at something, and when used properly aids in the communication process. What are some of the defects of the analogy Mathews uses? What are some differences between dictionaries and carpenters' squares? A square is a tool used by a carpenter; a dictionary is a tool used by a reader or writer. A carpenter makes things of wood, things that have substance; a reader studies, interprets, attempts to understand, works with abstract ideas. Here the two draw apart and seem unlike one another. But a carpenter also uses hammer, saw, and chisel; how does their use differ from that of the square? What we are attempting to do here is understand how Mathews can logically use such apparently disparate objects as a carpenter's square and a dictionary, using one to introduce the other. If he can do so logically he is likely to achieve greater and more immedite understanding; if he fails to do so logically he is going to make understanding even more difficult.

You may have learned something new about words long in your vocabulary from Mathews' essay. What did his information about "Jesus" tell you? What about "ostrich"? Note how the author points out the aid you can obtain from knowledge you already possess, even without consulting the dictionary, merely by acting like a dictionary, as in his discussion of "Mimus polyglottos." Try his system on "duodecimal," "hydromechanics," "monochrome," and "audiophile."

How to Read a Dictionary

MORTIMER ADLER

The dictionary invites a playful reading. It challenges anyone to sit down with it in an idle moment only to find an hour gone by without being bored. Recently I noticed an advertisement for a dictionary as a wonder book. "Astonished Actually Means Thunderstruck" was the headline, written obviously in the hope that the prospective buyer would be thunderstruck, or wonderstruck, enough to look further. And the rest of the ad listed such tidbits as a "*disaster* literally means 'the stars are against you!'" or "to tantalize is to torment with the punishment of Tantalus as told in Greek mythology."

While I do not think astonishment is the dictionary's main mission in life, I cannot resist reporting some of the things I learned accidentally while thumbing its pages, in the course of writing this article. I discovered that the word "solecism" derives from Soli, the name of a Greek colony in Cicilia, whose inhabitants were thought by the Athenians to speak bad Greek; hence, "solecism" was probably the equivalent in Greek slang for a Bostonian's contemptuous reference to "New Yorkese." I learned that "coal" originally meant charred wood. It was then applied to mineral coal when this was first introduced, under such names as "sea-coal" and "pit-coal." Now that mineral coal is the more common variety, we redundantly refer to charred wood as "charcoal." I was edified by the fact that the drink "Tom and Jerry" derives its name from the two chief characters in Egan's "Life of London" (1821), that in England a low beer joint is called a "Tom and Jerry Shop," and that indulgence in riotous behavior is called "to tom and jerry." I had always thought that a forlorn hope was really a hope on the verge of turning into despair, but it seems that it isn't a hope at all. "Hope" here is a misspelling of the Dutch word "hoop" meaning heap. A forlorn hope is a storming party, a band of heroes who are willing to end up in a heap for their country's cause. And most shocking of all was the discovery that one theory about the origin of the magician's "hocus pocus" accounts for it as a corruption of *"hoc est corpus"*—the sacred words accompanying the sacrament of the Eucharist. This, together with the reversal in meaning of "dunce"—from the proper name of Duns Scotus, the subtlest doctor of the Church, to naming a numbskull—provides a two word commentary on the transition from the Middle Ages to modern times.

The staid modern dictionary is full of such wit even when it doesn't try to be funny, as Dr. Johnson did when he defined "oats" as "a grain which in England is generally given to horses, but in Scotland supports the people." Look up "Welsh rabbit," for example, or "scotch capon" or "swiss steak," and you will discover gentle jokes about national shortcomings in diet.

I find that what interests me most of all are the shifts in meaning of common words in daily use. From meaning an attendant on horses, "marshall" has come to mean a leader of men; though also originating in the stable, "constable" has gone in the reverse direction from signifying an officer of highest rank to denoting a policeman; "boon" has done an about-face by becoming the gift which answers a petition, having been the prayer which asked for it; "magistrate" and "minister" have changed places with each other in the ups and downs of words, for in current political usage, "magistrate" usually names a minor official, whereas "minister" refers to a *major* diplomatic or cabinet post. It is often hard to remember that a minister is a *servant* of the people, and harder still to recall the precise point of religious controversy which caused the substitution of "minister" for "priest" as the name for one who served in the performance of sacerdotal functions. And readers of our Constitution should have their attention called to a shift in the word "citizen" from meaning any one who, by birth or choice, owes allegiance to the state, to the narrower designation of those who are granted the right to vote. Similarly, "commerce" has narrowed in meaning; like "trade," it once meant every dealing in merchandise, but now is distinguished from industry according to the difference between distributing commodities and producing them.

The word "commerce" reminds me of one other sort of incidental inquiry the dictionary lures you into. You discover that "commerce" and "mercenary" have the same root in *"mercis,"* wares, and that leads you to the closely related root *"merces,"* pay or reward, which is embodied in the word "mercy." If you start this game of research, you will find such roots as *"spec"* from *"spectare"* meaning to look at or see, which generates a family of 246 English words (species, speculate, specimen, specify, spectacle, inspect, respect, aspect, etc.); or *"press"* from *"primo"* meaning to squeeze, which has an equally large family (impress, repress, pressing, compress, suppress, oppress, depress, express, etc.).

It is almost as hard to stop writing about the dictionary in this way as to stop reading one when you are in hot pursuit of the mysteries of human speech. But, over and above such fascinations, the dictionary has its sober uses. To make the most of these one has to know how to read the special sort of book a dictionary is. But, before I state the rules, let me see if I can explain why most people today don't use dictionaries in a manner befitting the purpose for which they were originally intended.

In its various sizes and editions, the dictionary is an unlisted best-seller on every season's list. To be able to get along without one would be a sign of supreme literacy—of complete competence as a reader and writer. The dictionary exists, of course, because there is no one in that condition. But, if the dictionary is the necessity we all acknowledge, why is it so infrequently used by the man who owns one? And, even when we do consult it, why do most of us misuse the dictionary or use it poorly?

The answer to both questions may be that few of us make efforts at reading or writing anything above the present level of our literary competence. The books—or maybe it is just the newspapers and magazines—we read, and the things we write, don't send us to the dictionary for help. Our vocabularies are quite adequate, because the first rule in most contemporary writing is the taboo against strange words, or familiar words in strange senses.

Of course, there are always people (not excluding college graduates) who have difficulty with spelling or pronouncing even the common words in daily discourse. That, by the way, is the source of the most frequent impulse to go to the dictionary. There is nothing wrong about this. The dictionary is there to render this simple service—in fact, Noah Webster began his career as the compiler of a spelling book which sold in the millions. But my point remains—the dictionary has other and more important uses, and the reason we do not generally avail ourselves of these services is not our superiority, but rather our lack of need as the life of letters is currently lived.

The history of dictionaries, I think, will bear me out on this point. The Greeks did not have a dictionary, even though "lexicon" is the Greek word for it. They had no need for foreign language dictionaries because there was no literature in a foreign language they cared to read. They had no need for a Greek word-book because the small educated class already knew what such a book would contain. This small group of literate men would have been, like the modern French Academy, the makers of the dictionary, the arbiters of good usage. But at a time when so sharp a line separated the learned from the lewd (which, in an obsolete usage, means *unlettered*), there was no occasion for the few men who could make a dictionary to prepare one for the others.

George Santayana's remark about the Greeks—that they were the only uneducated people in European history—has a double significance. The masses were, of course, uneducated, but even the learned few were not educated in the sense that they had to sit at the feet of foreign masters. Education, in that sense, begins with the Romans, who went to school to Greek pedagogues, and became cultivated through contact with Greek culture. It is not surprising, therefore, that the first dictionaries were glossaries of Homeric words. The earliest lexicon which is still extant is such a glossary, prepared by a Greek, Apollonius, in the fifth century of our era, obviously intended to help Romans read the "Iliad" and "Odyssey" of Homer, as well as other Greek literature which employed the Homeric vocabulary. Most of us today need similar glossaries to read Shakespeare well.

There were dictionaries in the Middle Ages—a famous Latin one by the Spaniard, Isidore of Seville, which was really a philosophical work, a sort of encyclopedia of worldly knowledge accomplished by discussions of the most important technical terms occurring in learned discourse. There were foreign-language dictionaries in the Renaissance (both Latin and Greek) made necessary by the fact that the *humane letters* which dominated the education of the period were from the ancient languages. Even when the vulgar tongues—English, French, or Italian—gradually displaced Latin as the language of learning, the pursuit of learning was still the privilege of the few. Under such circumstances, dictionaries were intended for a limited audience, mainly as an aid to reading the most worthy literature. In attempting to compile a standard dictionary, Dr. Johnson derived his norms from the usage of the best writers, on the theory that this would furnish a guide to others who tried to read them, or who tried to write as well.

We see, then, that from the beginning the educational motive dominated the making of dictionaries, though, as in the case of Dr. Johnson, and the work of the French and Italian Academies, there was also an interest in preserving the purity and order of the language. As against the latter interest, the *Oxford English Dictionary*, begun in 1857, was a new departure, in that it did not try to dictate the best usage, but rather to present an accurate historical record of every type of usage—the worst as well as the best, taken from popular as well as stylish writing. But this conflict between the mission of the lexicographer as self-appointed arbiter and his function as historian can be regarded as a side-issue, for the dictionary, however constructed, is primarily an educational instrument. And the problem is whether that instrument is currently well used.

Our own Noah·Webster is in a sense the hero of the story. Alarmed by the state into which learning had fallen after the Revolutionary War, Webster sought to make a one volume dictionary which would serve in the self-education of the semiliterate masses. He was concerned with the masses, not the elite, and with self-education, at a time when this country had not yet become democratic enough to regard the public education of all its children as a primary obligation of the state. The Webster dictionary was probably one of the first self-help books to become a popular best-seller. And the paradox is that now, with public education widely established in this country, with "literacy" as universal as suffrage, the self-help potentialities of a dictionary are seldom realized by the millions who own one. I am not thinking merely of children from progressive schools who cannot use a dictionary because they do not know the alphabet. I am thinking of all the products of contemporary education who, not being taught or inspired to read the great and difficult books, have little use for the dictionary. *How much better educated was the self-read man whom Webster helped!*

This brief history of dictionaries is relevant to the rules for reading and using them well. One of the first rules as to how to read a book is to know what sort of book it is. That means knowing what the author's intention was and what sort of thing you can expect to find in his work. If you look upon a dictionary merely as a spelling book or a guide to pronunciation, you will use it accordingly. If you realize that it contains a wealth of historical information, crystallized in the growth of the language, you will pay attention, not merely to the variety of meanings which are listed above under each word, but to their order.

And above all if you are interested in advancing your own education, you will use a dictionary according to its primary intention —as a help in reading books that might otherwise be too difficult because their vocabulary includes technical words, archaic words, literary allusions, or even familiar words used in now obsolete senses. The number of words in a man's vocabulary is as definite as the number of dollars he has in the bank; equally definite is the number of senses in which a man is able to use any given word. But there is this difference: a man cannot draw upon the public treasury when his bank-balance is overdrawn. But we can all draw upon the dictionary to get the coin we need to carry on the transaction of reading anything we want to read.

Let me be sure that I am not misunderstood. I am not saying that a dictionary is all you need in order to move anywhere in the realms of literature. There are many problems to be solved, in reading a book well, other than those arising from the author's vocabulary. And even with respect to vocabulary, the dictionary's primary service is on those occasions when you are confronted with a technical word or with a word that is wholly new to you—such as "costard" (an apple), or "hoatzin" (a South American bird) or "rabato" (a kind of flaring collar). More frequently the problem of interpretation arises because a relatively familiar word seems to be used in a strange sense. Here the dictionary will help, but it will not solve the problem. The dictionary may suggest the variety of senses in which the troublesome word can be used, but it can never determine how the author you are reading used it. That you must decide by wrestling with the context. More often than not, especially with distinguished writers, the word may be given a special, an almost unique, shade of meaning. The growth of your own vocabulary, in the important dimension of multiple meanings as well as in mere quantity of words, will depend, first of all, upon the character of the books you read, and secondly, upon the use you make of the dictionary as a guide. You will misuse it—you will stultify rather than enlighten yourself—if you substitute the dictionary for the exercise of your own interpretative judgment in reading.

This suggests several other rules as to how *not* to read a dictionary. There is no more irritating fellow than the man who tries to settle an argument about communism, or justice, or liberty, by quoting from Webster. Webster and all his fellow lexicographers may be respected as authorities on word-usage, but they are not the ultimate founts of wisdom. They are no Supreme Court to which we can appeal for a decision of those fundamental controversies which, despite the warnings of semanticists, get us involved with abstract words. It is well to remember that the dictionary's authority can, for obvious reasons, be surer in the field of concrete words, and even in the field of the abstract technical words of science, than it ever can be with respect to philosophical words. Yet these words are indispensable if we are going to talk, read, or write about the things that matter most.

Another negative rule is: Don't swallow the dictionary. Don't try to get word-rich quick, by memorizing a lot of fancy words whose meanings are unconnected with any actual experience. Merely verbal knowledge is almost worse than no knowledge at all. If learning consisted in nothing but knowing the meanings of words, we could abolish all our courses of study, and substitute the dictionary for every other sort of book. But no one except a pedant or a fool would regard it as profitable or wise to read the dictionary from cover to cover.

In short, don't forget that the dictionary is a book about words, not about things. It can tell you how men have used words, but it does not define the nature of the things the words name. A Scandinavian university undertook a "linguistic experiment" to prove that human arguments always reduce to verbal differences. Seven lawyers were given seven dictionary definitions of truth and asked to defend them. They soon forgot to stick to the "verbal meanings" they had been assigned, and became vehemently involved in defending or opposing certain fundamental views about the nature of truth. The experiment showed that discussions may start about the meanings of words, but that, when interest in the problem is aroused, they seldom end there. Men pass from words to things, from names to natures. The dictionary can start an argument, but only thought or research can end it.

If we remember that a dictionary is a book about words, we can derive from that fact all the rules for reading a dictionary intelligently. Words can be looked at in four ways.

(1) *Words are physical things*—writable marks and speakable sounds. There must, therefore, be uniform ways of spelling and pronouncing them, though the uniformity is often spoiled by variations.

(2) *Words are parts of speech.* Each single word plays a grammatical role in the more complicated structure of a phrase or a sentence. According to the part it plays, we classify it as a certain part of speech—noun or verb, adjective or adverb, article or preposition. The same word can vary in different usages, shifting from one part of speech to another, as when we say "Man the boat" or "Take the jump." Another sort of grammatical variation in words arises from their inflection, but in a relatively uninflected language like English, we need to pay attention only to the conjugation of the verb (infinitive, participle, past tense, etc.), the case of the noun (singular and plural), and the degree of the adjective (especially the comparative and superlative).

(3) *Words are signs.* They have meanings, not one but many. These meanings are related in various ways. Sometimes they shade from one into another; sometimes one word will have two or more sets of totally unrelated meanings. Through their meanings words are related to one another—as synonyms sharing in the same meaning even though they differ in its shading; or as antonyms through opposition or contrast of meanings. Furthermore, it is in their capacity as signs that we distinguish words as proper or common names (according as they name just one thing or many which are alike in some respect); and as concrete or abstract names (according as they point to some thing which we can sense, or refer to some aspect of things which we can understand by thought but not observe through our senses).

Finally, (4) *words are conventional.* They mean or signify natural things, but they themselves are not natural. They are man-made signs. That is why every word has a history, just as everything else man makes has a time and place of origin, and a cultural career, in which it goes through certain transformations. The history of words is given by their etymological derivation from original word-roots, prefixes, and suffixes; it includes the account of their physical change, both in spelling and pronunciation; it tells of their shifting meanings, and which among them are archaic and obsolete, which are current and regular, which are idiomatic, colloquial, or slang.

A good dictionary will answer all your questions about words under these four heads. The art of reading a dictionary (as any other book) consists in knowing what questions to ask about words and how to find the answers. I have suggested the questions. The dictionary itself tells you how to find the answers. In this respect, it is a perfect self-help book, because it tells you what to pay attention to and how to interpret the various abbreviations and symbols it uses in giving you the four varieties of information about words. Anyone who fails to consult the explanatory notes and the list of abbreviations at the beginning of a dictionary can blame only himself for not being able to read the dictionary well. Unfortunately, many people fail here, as in the case of other books, because they insist upon neglecting the prefatory matter—as if the author were just amusing himself by including it.

I think these suggestions about how to read, and how not to misuse, a dictionary are easy to follow. But like all other rules they will be followed well only by the man who is rightly motivated in the first place. And, in the last place, they will be wisely applied only by the man who remembers that we are both *free* and *bound* in all our dealings with language, whether as writers or readers.

"When I use a word," Humpty-Dumpty said in a rather scornful tone, "it means just what I choose it to mean—neither more nor less."

"The question is," said Alice, "whether you can make words mean so many different things."

"The question is," said Humpty-Dumpty, "which is to be master— that's all."

DISCUSSION

In his essay Mortimer Adler makes some nice distinctions and uses words in unusual but accurate senses. An example is his quotation of George Santayana's remark that the Greeks were the only uneducated people in European history. We have all been taught the greatness of Greek culture; how can Santayana call them uneducated? Note Adler's use of "lewd" in the previous paragraph; what is he illustrating?

Adler says that Noah Webster's aim in writing his famous dictionary differed significantly from the aim of previous lexicographers; what was his difference? Some observers would say that Webster's aim was in keeping with the American tradition; what would they mean by such a statement? What is the primary intention of the dictionary, according to Adler? Do you agree? What does Adler tell us about how not to read a dictionary? Do you understand his statement that "the dictionary can start an argument, but only thought or research can end it"? How can the dictionary start an argument?

Sabotage in Springfield

WILSON FOLLETT

Of dictionaries, as of newspapers, it might be said that the bad ones are too bad to exist, the good ones too good not to be better. No dictionary of a living language is perfect or ever can be, if only because the time required for compilation, editing, and issuance is so great that shadows of obsolescence are falling on parts of any such work before it ever gets into the hands of a user. Preparation of *Webster's Third New International Dictionary of the English Language* began intensively in the Springfield establishment of G. & C. Merriam Company in 1936, but the century was nine months into its seventh decade before any outsider could have his first look at what had been accomplished. His first look is, of course, incompetent to acquaint him with the merits of the new work; these no one can fully discover without months or years of everyday use. On the other hand, it costs only minutes to find out that what will rank as the great event of American linguistic history in this decade, and perhaps in this quarter century, is in many crucial particulars a very great calamity.

Why should the probable and possible superiorities of the Third New International be so difficult to assess, the shortcomings so easy? Because the superiorities are special, departmental, and recondite, the shortcomings general and within the common grasp. The new dictionary comes to us with a claim of 100,000 new words or new definitions. These run almost overwhelmingly to scientific and technological terms or meanings that have come into existence since 1934, and especially to words classified as ISV (belonging to the international scientific vocabulary). No one person can possibly use or even comprehend all of them; the coverage in this domain, certainly impressive to the non-specialist, may or may not command the admiration of specialists. It is said that historians of the graphic arts and of architecture were displeased with the 1934 Webster, both for its omissions and for some defintions of what is included in their fields. Its 1961 successor may have disarmed their reservations; only they can pronounce.

But all of us may without brashness form summary judgments about the treatment of what belongs to all of us—the standard, staple, traditional language of general reading and speaking, the ordinary vocabulary and idioms of novelist, essayist, letter writer, reporter, editorial writer, teacher, student, advertiser; in short, fundamental English. And it is precisely in this province that Webster III has thrust upon us a dismaying assortment of the questionable, the perverse, the unworthy, and the downright outrageous.

Furthermore, what was left out is as legitimate a grievance to the ordinary reader as anything that has been put in. Think—if you can—of an unabridged dictionary from which you cannot learn who Mark Twain was (though *mark twain* is entered as a leadsman's cry), or what were the names of the apostles, or that the Virgin was Mary the mother of Jesus of Nazareth, or what and where the District of Columbia is!

The disappointment and the shock are intensified of course, because of the unchallenged position earned by the really unabridged immediate predecessor of this strange work. *Webster's New International Dictionary,* Second Edition (1934), consummated under the editorship of William Allan Neilson, at once became the most important reference book in the world to American writers, editors, teachers, students, and general readers—everyone to whom American English was a matter of serious interest. What better could the next revision do than extend the Second Edition in the direction of itself, bring it up to date, and correct its scattering of oversights and errata?

The 1934 dictionary had been, heaven knows, no citadel of conservatism, no last bastion of puristical bigotry. But it had made shrewd reports on the status of individual words; it had taken its clear, beautifully written definitions from fit uses of an enormous vocabulary by judicious users; it had provided accurate, impartial accounts of the endless guerrilla war between grammarian and antigrammarian and so given every consultant the means to work out his own decisions. Who could wish the forthcoming revision any better fortune than a comparable success in applying the same standards to whatever new matter the new age imposed?

Instead, we have seen a century and a third of illustrious history largely jettisoned; we have seen a novel dictionary formula improvised, in great part out of snap judgments and the sort of theoretical improvement that in practice impairs; and we have seen the gates propped wide open in enthusiastic hospitality to miscellaneous confusions and corruptions. In fine, the anxiously awaited work that was to have crowned cisatlantic linguistic scholarship with a particular glory turns out to be a scandal and a disaster. Worse yet, it plumes itself on its faults and parades assiduously cultivated sins as virtues without precedent.

Examination cannot proceed far without revealing that Webster III, behind its front of passionless objectivity, is in truth a fighting document. And the enemy it is out to destroy is every obstinate vestige of linguistic punctilio, every surviving influence that makes for the upholding of standards, every criterion for distinguishing between better usages and worse. In other words, it has gone over bodily to the school that construes traditions as enslaving, the rudimentary principles of syntax as crippling, and taste as irrelevant. This resolution leaves it in the anomalous position of loudly glorifying its own ancestry—which is indeed glorious—while tacitly sabotaging the principles and ideals that brought the preceding Merriam-Webster to its unchallengeable preeminence. The Third New International is at once a resounding tribute of lip service to the Second and a wholesale repudiation of it—a sweeping act of apology, contrition, and reform.

The right-about-face is, of course, particularly evident in the vocabulary approved. Within a few days of publication the new dictionary was inevitably notorious for its unreserved acceptance as standard of *wise up, get hep* (it uses the second as a definition of the first), *ants in one's pants, one for the book; hugeous, nixie, passel, hepped up* (with *hepcat* and *hepster*), *anyplace, someplace,* and so forth. These and a swarm of their kind it admits to full canonical standing by the suppression of such qualifying status labels as *colloquial, slang, cant, facetious,* and *substandard.* The classification *colloquial* it abolishes outright: "it is impossible to know whether a word out of context is colloquial or not." Of *slang* it makes a chary occasional use despite a similar reservation: "No word is invariably slang, and many standard words can be given slang connotations or used so inappropriately as to become slang." *Cornball* is ranked as slang, *corny* is not.

The overall effect signifies a large-scale abrogation of one major responsibility of the lexicographer. He renounces it on the curious ground that helpful discriminations are so far beyond his professional competence that he is obliged to leave them to those who, professing no competence at all, have vainly turned to him for guidance. If some George Ade of the future, aspiring to execute a fable in slang, were to test his attempt by the status labels in Webster III, he would quickly discover with chagrin that he had expressed himself almost without exception in officially applauded English. With but slight exaggeration we can say that if an expression can be shown to have been used in print by some jaded reporter, some candidate for office or his speech writer, some pot-boiling minor novelist, it is well enough credentialed for the full blessing of the new lexicography.

This extreme tolerance of crude neologisms and of shabby diction generally, however, is but one comparatively trifling aspect of the campaign against punctilio. We begin to sound its deeper implications when we plunge into the definitions and the copious examples that illustrate and support them. Under the distributive pronoun *each* we find, side by side: "(each of them is to pay his own fine) (each of them are to pay their own fine)." Where could anyone look for a neater, more succinct way to outlaw the dusty dogma that a pronoun should agree in number with its antecedent? Here is the same maneuver again under another distributive, *everybody:* "usu. referred to by the third person singular (everybody is bringing his own lunch) but sometimes by a plural personal prounoun (everybody had made up their minds)." Or try *whom* and *whomever:* "(a ... recruit whom he hoped would prove to be a crack salesman) (people ... whom you never thought would sympathize) ... (I go out to talk to whomever it is) ... (he attacked whomever disagreed with him)." It is, then,

all right to put the subject of a finite verb in the accusative case—
"esp. after a preposition or a verb of which it might mistakenly be
considered the object."

Shall we look into what our dictionary does with a handful of
the more common solecisms, such as a publisher might introduce
into a cooked-up test for would-be copy editors? Begin with
center around (or *about*). It seems obvious that expressions derived from Euclidean geometry should make Euclidean sense. A
center is a point; it is what things are around, not what is around
them; they center *in* or *on* or *at* the point. The Second Edition
defined the Great White Way as "That part of Broadway . . .
centering about Times Square"—patently an oversight. Is it the
same oversight that produces, in the Third: *heresy . . . 3:* a group
or school of thought centering around a particular heresy?" We
look up *center* itself, and, lo: "(a story to tell, centered around
the political development of a great state) . . . (more scholarship
than usual was centered around the main problems)," followed
by several equivalent specimens.

Here is *due to*. First we come on irreproachable definitions, irre-
proachably illustrated, of *due* noun and *due* adjective, and we
think we are out of the woods. Alas, they are followed by the
manufacture of a composite preposition, *due to*, got up solely to
extenuate such abominations as "the event was canceled due to
inclement weather." An adjective can modify a verb, then. And
here is a glance at that peculiarly incriminating redundancy of
slipshod writer, *equally as:* "equally opposed to Communism as to
Fascism." The intolerable *hardly than* or *scarcely than* construction is in full favor: "hardly had the birds dropped than she
jumped into the water and retrieved them." The sequence *different
than* has the double approbation of editorial use and a citation:
conjunctive *unlike* means "in a manner that is different than,"
and a passage under *different* reads "vastly different in size than
it was twenty-five years ago." Adjectival *unlike* and conjunctive
unlike both get illustrations that implicitly commend the unan-
chored and grammarless modifier: "so many fine men were outside
the charmed circle that, unlike most colleges, there was no disgrace in not being a club man;" "unlike in the gasoline engine, fuel
does not enter the cylinder with air on the intake stroke."

This small scattering should not end without some notice of that darling of the advanced libertarians, *like* as a conjunction, first in the meaning of *as*, secondly (and more horribly) in that of *as if*. Now, it is well known to the linguistic historian that *like* was so used for a long time before and after Langland. But it is as well known that the language rather completely sloughed off this usage; that it has long been no more than a regional colloquialism, a rarely seen aberration among competent writers, or an artificially cultivated irritant among defiant ones. The *Saturday Evening Post*, in which *like* for *as* is probably more frequent than in any other painstakingly edited magazine, has seldom if ever printed that construction except in reproducing the speech or tracing the thoughts of characters to whom it might be considered natural. The arguments for *like* have been merely defensive and permissive. Not for centuries has there been any real pressure of authority on a writer to use *like* as a conjunction—until our Third New International Dictionary decided to exert its leverage.

How it is exerted will appear in the following: "(impromptu programs where they ask questions much like I do on the air) . . . (looks like they can raise better tobacco) (looks like he will get the job) (wore his clothes like he was . . . afraid of getting dirt on them) (was like he'd come back from a long trip) (acted like she felt sick) . . . (sounded like the motor had stopped) . . . (the violin now sounds like an old masterpiece should) (did it like he told me to) . . . (wanted a doll like she saw in the store window) . . . (anomalies like just had occurred)."

By the process represented in the foregoing and countless others for which there is no room here, the latest Webster whittles away at one after another of the traditionary controls until there is little or nothing left of them. The controls, to be sure, have often enough been overvalued and overdone by pedants and purists, by martinets and bigots; but more often, and much more importantly, they have worked as aids toward dignified, workmanlike, and cogent uses of the wonderful language that is our inheritance. To erode and undermine them is to convert the language into a confusion of unchanneled, incalculable williwaws, a capricious wind blowing whithersoever it listeth. And that, if we are to judge by the total effect of the pages under scrutiny—2720 of them and nearly 8000 columns of vocabulary, all compact in Times roman—is exactly what is wanted by the patient and dedicated saboteurs in Springfield. They, if they keep their ears to the ground, will hear many echoes of the despairing cry already wrung from one editorial assistant on a distinguished magazine that still puts its faith in standards: "Why have a Dictionary at all if anything goes?"

The definitions are reinforced, it will have been conveyed, with copious citations from printed sources. These citations occupy a great fraction of the total space. They largely account for the reduction in the number of entries (from 600,000 to 450,000) and for the elimination of the Gazetteer, the Biographical Dictionary, and the condensed key to pronunciation and symbols that ran across the bottoms of facing pages—all very material deprivations. Some 14,000 authors, we are told, are represented in the illustrative quotations—"mostly from the mid-twentieth century."

Can some thousands of authors truly worth space in a dictionary ever be found in any one brief period? Such a concentration can hardly fail to be, for the purposes of a dictionary, egregiously overweighted with the contemporary and the transient. Any very short period, such as a generation, is a period of transition in the history of English, and any great mass of examples drawn primarily from it will be disproportionately focused on transitional and ephemeral elements. To say that recording English *as we find it today* is precisely the purpose of a new dictionary is not much of a retort. For the bulk of the language that we use has come down to us with but minor, glacially slow changes from time out of mind, and a worthy record of it must stand on a much broader base than the fashions of yesterday.

It is, then, a mercy that among the thousands of scraps from recent authors, many of them still producing, we can also find hundreds from Shakespeare, the English Bible, Fielding, Dickens, Hawthorne, Melville, Henry James, Mark Twain, and so on. But the great preponderance of latter day prose, little of it worth repeating and a good deal of it hardly worth printing in the first place, is likely to curtail by years the useful life of the Third New International.

So much is by the way. When we come to the definitions proper we face something new, startling, and formidable in lexicography. The definitions, all of them conformed to a predetermined rhetorical pattern, may be products of a theory—Gestaltist, perhaps?—of how the receiving mind works. The pattern, in the editor's general preface, is described as follows: "The primary objective of precise, sharp defining has been met through development of a new dictionary style based upon completely analytical one-phrase definitions throughout the book. Since the headword in a definition is intended to be modified only by structural elements restrictive in some degree and essential to each other, the use of commas either to separate or to group has been severely limited, chiefly to elements in apposition or in series. The new defining pattern does not provide for a predication which conveys further expository comment."

This doctrine of the strictly unitary definition is of course formulated and applied in the interests of a local integrity and a simplification never before consistently attained by lexical definitions. What it produces, when applied with the rigor here insisted on, is in the first place some of the oddest prose ever concocted by pundits. A typical specimen, from the definition of the simplest possible term: "*rabbit punch* . . . : a short chopping blow delivered to the back of the neck or the base of the skull with the edge of the hand opposite the thumb that is illegal in boxing." When the idea, being not quite so simple, requires the one-phrase statement of several components, the definition turns out to be a great unmanageable and unpunctuated blob of words strung out beyond the retentive powers of most minds that would need the definition at all. Both theory and result will emerge clearly enough from a pair of specimens, the first dealing with a familiar everyday noun, the second with a mildly technical one:

groan . . . *1:* a deep usu. inarticulate and involuntary often strangled sound typically abruptly begun and ended and usu. indicative of pain or grief or tension or desire or sometimes disapproval or annoyance.

kymograph . . . *1:* a recording device including an electric motor or clockwork that drives a usu. slowly revolving drum which carries a roll of plain or smoked paper and also having an arrangement for tracing on the paper by means of a stylus a graphic record of motion or pressure (as of the organs of speech, blood pressure, or respiration) often in relation to particular intervals of time.

About these typical definitions as prose, there is much that any good reader might well say. What must be said is that the grim suppression of commas is a mere crotchet. It takes time to read such definitions anyway; commas in the right places would speed rather than slow the reading and would clarify rather than obscure the sense, so that the unitary effect—largely imaginary at best—would be more helped than hurt. In practice, the one-phrase design without further expository predication lacks all the asserted advantages over a competently written definition of the free conventional sort; it is merely more difficult to write, often impossible to write well, and tougher to take in. Compare the corresponding definitions from the Second Edition:

groan . . . A low, moaning sound; usually, a deep, mournful sound uttered in pain or great distress; sometimes, an expression of strong disapprobation; as, the remark was received with *groans.*

kymograph . . . *a* An automatic apparatus consisting of a motor revolving a drum covered with smoked paper, on which curves of pressure, etc., may be traced.

Everyone professionally concerned with the details of printed English can be grateful to the new Webster for linking the parts of various expressions that have been either hyphenated compounds or separate words—*highlight, highbrow* and *lowbrow, overall, wisecrack, lowercase* and *uppercase,* and so on. Some of the unions now recognized were long overdue; many editors have already got them written into codes of house usage. But outside this small province the new work is a copy editor's despair, a propounder of endless riddles.

What, for example, are we to make of the common abbreviations *i.e.* and *e.g.?* The first is entered in the vocabulary as *ie* (no periods, no space), the second as *e g* (space, no periods). In the preliminary list, "Abbreviations Used in This Dictionary," both are given the customary periods. (Oddly, the list translates its *i.e.* into "that is," but merely expands *e.g.* into "exempli gratia.") Is one to follow the vocabulary or the list? What point has the seeming inconsistency?

And what about capitalization? All vocabulary entries are in lowercase except for such abbreviations as ARW (air raid warden), MAB (medical advisory board), and PX (post exchange). Words possibly inviting capitalization are followed by such injunctions as *cap, usu cap, sometimes not cap, usu cap 1st A, usu cap A&B.* (One of the small idiosyncrasies is that "usu.," the most frequent abbreviation, is given a period when roman, denied it when italic.) From *america,* adjective—all proper nouns are excluded—to *american yew* there are over 175 consecutive entries that require such injunctions; would it not have been simpler and more economical to capitalize the entries? A flat *"cap,"* of course, means "always capitalized." But how often is "usually," and when is "sometimes"? We get dictionaries expressly that they may settle such problems for us. This dictionary seems to make a virtue of leaving them in flux, with the explanation that many matters are subjective and that the individual must decide them for himself— a curious abrogation of authority in a work extolled as "more useful and authoritative than any previous dictionary."

The rock-bottom practical truth is that the lexicographer cannot abrogate his authority if he wants to. He may think of himself as a detached scientist reporting the facts of language, declining to recommend use of anything or abstention from anything; but the myriad consultants of his work are not going to see him so. He helps create, not a book of fads and fancies and private opinions, but a Dictionary of the English Lanuage. It comes to every reader under auspices that say, not "Take it or leave it," but rather something like this: "Here in 8000 columns is a definitive report of what a synod of the most trustworthy American experts consider the English language to be in the seventh decade of the twentieth century. This is your language; take it and use it. And if you use it in conformity with the principles and practices here exemplified, your use will be the most accurate attainable by any American of this era." The fact that the compilers disclaim authority and piously refrain from judgments is meaningless; the work itself, by virtue of its inclusions and exclusions, its mere existence, is a whole universe of judgments, received by millions as the Word from on high.

And there we have the reason why it is so important for the dictionary maker to keep his discriminations sharp, why it is so damaging if he lets them get out of working order. Suppose he enters a new definition for no better reason than that some care-less, lazy or uninformed scribbler has jumped to an absurd con-clusion about what a word means or has been too harrassed to run down the word he really wanted. This new definition is going to persuade tens of thousands that, say, *cohort,* a word of multi-tude, means one associate or crony "(he and three alleged house-breaking cohorts were arraigned on attempted burglary charges)" or that the vogue word *ambivalence,* which denotes simultaneous love and hatred of someone or something, means "continual os-cillation between one thing and its opposite (novels ... vitiated by an ambivalence between satire and sentimentalism)." To what is the definer contributing if not to subversion and decay? To the swallower of the definition it never occurs that he can have drunk corruption from a well that he has every reason to trust as the ultimate in purity. Multiply him by the number of people simul-taneously influenced, and the resulting figure by the years through which the influence continues, and a great deal of that product by the influences that will be disseminated through speech and writing, and you begin to apprehend the scope of the really enormous disaster that can and will be wrought by the lexicog-rapher's abandonment of his responsibility.

DISCUSSION

How would you assess Follett's position? What does he seem to want from a dictionary? Why does he call *Webster's Third* a "great calamity"? List the specific objections he has to the new edition; how well does he establish his case for each?

Follett's essay is really a book review that appeared in *The Atlantic Monthly;* does it read like a book review? What makes it a particular sort of book review?

Consider the opening of the third paragraph; what does it mean; do you agree?

But What's a Dictionary For?

BERGEN EVANS

The storm of abuse in the popular press that greeted the appearance of *Webster's Third New International Dictionary* is a curious phenomenon. Never has a scholarly work of this stature been attacked with such unbridled fury and contempt. An article in the *Atlantic* viewed it as a "disappointment," a "shock," a "calamity," "a scandal and a disaster." The New York *Times,* in a special editorial, felt that the work would "accelerate the deterioration" of the language and sternly accused the editors of betraying a public trust. The *Journal* of the American Bar Association saw the publication as "deplorable," "a flagrant example of lexicographic irresponsibility," "a serious blow to the cause of good English." *Life* called it "a non-word deluge," "monstrous," "abominable," and "a cause for dismay." They doubted that "Lincoln could have modelled his Gettysburg Address" on it—a concept of how things get written that throws very little light on Lincoln but a great deal on *Life.*

What underlies all this sound and fury? Is the claim of the G. & C. Merriam Company, probably the world's greatest dictionary maker, that the preparation of the work cost $3.5 million, that it required the efforts of three hundred scholars over a period of twenty-seven years, working on the largest collection of citations ever assembled in any language—is all this a fraud, a hoax?

So monstrous a discrepancy in evaluation requires us to examine basic principles. Just what's a dictionary for? What does it propose to do? What does the common reader go to a dictionary to find? What has the purchaser of a dictionary a right to expect for his money?

Before we look at basic principles, it is necessary to interpose two brief statements. The first of these is that a dictionary is concerned with words. Some have tables of weights and measures on the flyleaves. Some list historical events, and some, home remedies. And there's nothing wrong with their so doing. But the great increase in our vocabulary in the past three decades compels all dictionaries to make more efficient use of their space. And if something must be eliminated, it is sensible to throw out these extraneous things and stick to words,

Yet wild wails arose. The *Saturday Review* lamented that one can no longer find the goddess Astarte under a separate heading—though they point out that a genus of mollusks named after the goddess is included! They seemed to feel that out of sheer perversity the editors of the dictionary stooped to mollusks while ignoring goddesses and that, in some way, this typifies modern lexicography. Mr. Wilson Follett, folletizing (his mental processes demand some special designation) in the *Atlantic,* cried out in horror that one is not even able to learn from the Third International "that the Virgin was Mary the mother of Jesus!"

The second brief statement is that there has been even more progress in the making of dictionaries in the past thirty years than there has been in the making of automobiles. The difference, for example, between the much-touted Second International (1934) and the much-clouted Third International (1961) is not like the difference between yearly models but like the difference between the horse and buggy and the automobile. Between the appearance of these two editions a whole new science related to the making of dictionaries, the science of descriptive linguistics, has come into being.

Modern linguistics gets its charter from Leonard Bloomfield's *Language* (1933). Bloomfield, for thirteen years professor of Germanic philology at the University of Chicago and for nine years professor of linguistics at Yale, was one of those inseminating scholars who can't be relegated to any department and don't dream of accepting established categories and procedures just because they're established. He was as much an anthropologist as a linguist, and his concepts of language were shaped not by Strunk's *Elements of Style* but by his knowledge of Cree Indian dialects.

The broad general findings of the new science are:

1. All languages are systems of human conventions, not systems of natural laws. The first—and essential—step in the study of any language is observing and setting down precisely what happens when native speakers speak it.

2. Each language is unique in its pronunciation, grammar, and vocabulary. It cannot be described in terms of logic or of some theoretical, ideal language. It cannot be described in terms of any other language or even in terms of its own past.

3. All languages are dynamic rather than static, and hence a "rule" in any language can only be a statement of contemporary practice. Change is constant—and normal.

4. "Correctness" can rest only upon usage, for the simple reason that there is nothing else for it to rest on. And all usage is relative.

From these propositions it follows that a dictionary is good only insofar as it is a comprehensive and accurate description of current usage. And to be comprehensive it must include some indication of social and regional associations.

New dictionaries are needed because English has changed more in the past two generations than at any other time in its history. It has had to adapt to extraordinary cultural and technological changes, two world wars, unparalleled changes in transportation and communication, and unprecedented movements of populations.

More subtly, but pervasively, it has changed under the influence of mass education and the growth of democracy. As written English is used by increasing millions and for more reasons than ever before, the language has become more utilitarian and more informal. Every publication in America today includes pages that would appear, to the purist of forty years ago, unbuttoned gibberish. Not that they are; they simply show that you can't hold the language of one generation up as a model for the next.

It's not that you mustn't. You *can't*. For example, in the issue in which *Life* stated editorially that it would follow the Second International, there were over forty words, constructions, and meanings which are in the Third International but not in the Second. The issue of the New York *Times* which hailed the Second International as the authority to which it would adhere and the

Third International as a scandal and a betrayal which it would reject used one hundred and fifty-three separate words, phrases, and constructions which are listed in the Third International but not in the Second and nineteen others which are condemned in the Second. Many of them are used many times, more than three hundred such uses in all. The Washington *Post,* in an editorial captioned "Keep Your Old Webster's," says, in the first sentence, "don't throw it away," and in the second, "hang on to it." But the old Webster's labels *don't* "colloquial" and doesn't include "hang on to," in this sense, at all.

In short, all of these publications are written in the language that the Third International describes, even the very editorials which scorn it. And this is no coincidence, because the Third International isn't setting up any new standards at all; it is simply describing what *Life,* the Washington *Post,* and the New York *Times* are doing. Much of the dictionary's material comes from these very publications, the *Times,* in particular, furnishing more of its illustrative quotations than any other newspaper.

And the papers have no choice. No journal or periodical could sell a single issue today if it restricted itself to the American language of twenty-eight years ago. It couldn't discuss half the things we are interested in, and its style would seem stiff and cumbrous. If the editorials were serious, the public—and the stockholders—have reason to be grateful that the writers on these publications are more literate than the editors.

And so back to our questions: what's a dictionary for, and how, in 1962, can it best do what it ought to do? The demands are simple. The common reader turns to a dictionary for information about the spelling, pronunciation, meaning, and proper use of words. He wants to know what is current and respectable. But he wants—and has a right to—the truth, the full truth. And the full truth about any language, and especially about American English today, is that there are many areas in which certainty is impossible and simplification is misleading.

Even in so settled a matter as spelling, a dictionary cannot always be absolute. *Theater* is correct, but so is *theatre.* And so are *traveled* and *travelled, plow* and *plough, catalog* and *catalogue,* and scores of other variants. The reader may want a single certainty. He may have taken an unyielding position in an argument, he may have wagered in support of his conviction and may demand that the dictionary "settle" the matter. But neither his vanity nor his purse is any concern of the dictionary's; it must record the facts. And the fact here is that there are many words in our language which may be spelled, with equal correctness, in either of two ways.

So with pronunciation. A citizen listening to his radio might notice that James B. Conant, Bernard Baruch, and Dwight D. Eisenhower pronounce *economics* as ECKuhnomiks, while A. Whitney Griswold, Adlai Stevenson, and Herbert Hoover pronounce it EEKuhnomiks. He turns to the dictionary to see which of the two pronunciations is "right" and finds that they are both acceptable.

Has he been betrayed? Has the dictionary abdicated its responsibility? Should it say that one *must* speak like the president of Harvard or like the president of Yale, like the thirty-first President of the United States or like the thirty-fourth? Surely it's none of its business to make a choice. Not because of the distinction of these particular speakers; lexicography, like God, is no respecter of persons. But because so widespread and conspicuous a use of two pronunciations among people of this elevation shows that there *are* two pronunciations. Their speaking establishes the fact which the dictionary must record.

Among the "enormities" with which *Life* taxes the Third International is its listing of "the common mispronunciation" *heighth.* That it is labeled a "dialectal variant" seems, somehow, to compound the felony. But one hears the word so pronounced, and if one professes to give a full account of American English in the 1960s, one has to take some cognizance of it. All people do not possess *Life's* intuitive perception that the word is so "monstrous" that even to list it as a dialect variation is to merit scorn. Among these, by the way, was John Milton, who, in one of the greatest passages in all literature, besought the Holy Spirit to raise him to the "highth" of his great argument. And even the *Oxford English Dictionary* is so benighted as to list it, in full boldface, right alongside of *Height* as a variant that has been in the language since at least 1290.

Now there are still, apparently, millions of Americans who retain, in this as in much else, some of the speech of Milton. This particular pronunciation seems to be receding, but the *American Dialect Dictionary* still records instances of it from almost every state on the Eastern seaboard and notes that it is heard from older people and "occasionally in educated speech," "common with good speakers," "general," "widespread."

Under these circumstances, what is a dictionary to do? Since millions speak the word this way, the pronunciation can't be ignored. Since it has been in use as long as we have any record of English and since it has been used by the greatest writers, it can't be described as substandard or slang. But it is heard now only in certain localities. That makes it a dialectal pronunciation, and an honest dictionary will list it as such. What else can it do? Should it do?

The average purchaser of a dictionary uses it most often, probably, to find out what a word "means." As a reader, he wants to know what an author intended to convey. As a speaker or writer, he wants to know what a word will convey to his auditors. And this, too, is complex, subtle, and forever changing.

An illustration is furnished by an editorial in the Washington *Post* (January 17, 1962). After a ringing appeal to those who "love truth and accuracy" and the usual bombinations about "abdication of authority" and "barbarism," the editorial charges the Third International with "pretentious and obscure verbosity" and specifically instances its definition of "so simple an object as a door."

The definition reads:

a movable piece of firm material or a structure supported usu. along one side and swinging on pivots or hinges, sliding along a groove, rolling up and down, revolving as one of four leaves, or folding like an accordion by means of which an opening may be closed or kept open for passage into or out of a building, room, or other covered enclosure or a car, airplane, elevator, or other vehicle.

Then follows a series of special meanings, each particularly defined and, where necessary, illustrated by a quotation.

Since, aside from roaring and admonishing the "gentlemen from Springfield" that "accuracy and brevity are virtues," the *Post's* editorial fails to explain what is wrong with the definition, we can only infer from "so simple" a thing that the writer takes the plain, downright, man-in-the-street attitude that a door is a door and any damn fool knows that.

But if so, he has walked into one of lexicography's biggest booby traps: the belief that the obvious is easy to define. Whereas the opposite is true. Anyone can give a fair description of the strange, the new, or the unique. It's the commonplace, the habitual, that challenges definition, for its very commonness compels us to define it in uncommon terms. Dr. Johnson was ridiculed on just this score when his dictionary appeared in 1755. For two hundred years his definition of a network as "any thing reticulated or decussated, at equal distances, with interstices between the intersections" has been good for a laugh. But in the merriment one thing is always overlooked: no one has yet come up with a better definition! Subsequent dictionaries defined it as a mesh and then defined a mesh as a network. That's simple, all right.

Anyone who attempts sincerely to state what the word *door* means in the United States of America today can't take refuge in a log cabin. There has been an enormous prolifieration of closing and demarking devices and structures in the past twenty years, and anyone who tries to thread his way through the many meanings now included under *door* may have to sacrifice brevity to accuracy and even have to employ words that a limited vocabulary may find obscure.

Is the entrance to a tent a door, for instance? And what of the thing that seals the exit of an airplane? Is this a door? Or what of those sheets and jets of air that are now being used, in place of old-fashioned oak and hinges, to screen entrances and exits. Are they doors? And what of those accordion-like things that set off various sections of many modern apartments? The fine print in the lease takes it for granted that they are doors and that spaces demarked by them are rooms—and the rent is computed on the number of rooms.

Was I gypped by the landlord when he called the folding contraption that shuts off my kitchen a door? I go to the Second International, which the editor of the *Post* urges me to use in preference to the Third International. Here I find that a door is

> The movable frame or barrier of boards, or other material, usually turning on hinges or pivots or sliding, by which an entranceway into a house or apartment is closed and opened; also, a similar part of a piece of furniture, as in a cabinet or bookcase.

This is only forty-six words, but though it includes the cellar door, it excludes the barn door and the accordion-like thing.

So I go on to the Third International. I see at once that the new definition is longer. But I'm looking for accuracy, and if I must sacrifice brevity to get it, then I must. And, sure enough, in the definition which raised the *Post*'s blood pressure, I find the words "folding like an accordion." The thing *is* a door, and my landlord is using the word in one of its currently accepted meanings.

We don't turn to a work of reference merely for confirmation. We all have words in our vocabularies which we have misunderstood, and to come on the true meaning of one of these words is quite a shock. All our complacency and self-esteem rise to oppose the discovery. But eventually we must accept the humiliation and laugh it off as best we can.

Some, often those who have set themselves up as authorities, stick to their error and charge the dictionary with being in a conspiracy against them. They are sure that their meaning is the only "right" one. And when the dictionary doesn't bear them out they complain about "permissive" attitudes instead of correcting their mistake.

The New York *Times* and the *Saturday Review* both regarded as contemptibly "permissive" the fact that one meaning of one word was illustrated by a quotation from Polly Adler. But a rudimentary knowledge of the development of any language would have told them that the underworld has been a far more active force in shaping and enriching speech than all the synods that have ever convened. Their attitude is like that of the patriot who canceled his subscription to the *Dictionary of American Biography* when he discovered that the very first volume included Benedict Arnold!

The ultimate of "permissiveness," singled out by almost every critic for special scorn, was the inclusion in the Third International of *finalize*. It was this, more than any other one thing, that was given as the reason for sticking to the good old Second International—that "peerless authority on American English," as the *Times* called it. But if it was such an authority, why didn't they look into it? They would have found *finalize* if they had.

And why shouldn't it be there? It exists. It's been recorded for two generations. Millions employ it every day. Two Presidents of the United States—men of widely differing cultural backgrounds —have used it in formal statements. And so has the Secretary-General of the United Nations, a man of unusual linguistic attainment. It isn't permitting the word but omitting it that would break faith with the reader. Because it is exactly the sort of word we want information about.

To list it as substandard would be to imply that it is used solely by the ignorant and the illiterate. But this would be a misrepresentation: President Kennedy and U Thant are highly educated men, and both are articulate and literate. It isn't even a freak form. On the contrary, it is a classic example of a regular process of development in English, a process which has given us such thoroughly accepted words as *generalize, minimize, formalize,* and *verbalize.* Nor can it be dismissed on logical grounds or on the ground that it is a mere duplication of *complete.* It says something that *complete* doesn't say and says it in a way that is significant in the modern bureaucratic world: one usually *completes* something which he has initiated but *finalizes* the work of others.

One is free to dislike the word. I don't like it. But the editor of a dictionary has to examine the evidence for a word's existence and seek it in context to get, as clearly and closely as he can, the exact meaning that it conveys to those who use it. And if it is widely used by well-educated, literate, reputable people, he must list it as a standard word. He is not compiling a volume of his own prejudices.

An individual's use of his native tongue is the surest index to his position within his community. And those who turn to a dictionary expect from it some statement of the current status of a word or a grammatical construction. And it is with the failure to assume this function that modern lexicography has been most fiercely charged. The charge is based on a naïve assumption that simple labels can be attached in all instances. But they can't. Some words are standard in some constructions and not in others. There may be as many shades of status as of meaning, and modern lexicography instead of abdicating this function has fulfilled it to a degree utterly unknown to earlier dictionaries.

Consider the word *fetch,* meaning to "go get and bring to." Until recently a standard word of full dignity ("Fetch me, I pray thee, a little water in a vessel"—I Kings 17:10), it has become slightly tainted. Perhaps the command latent in it is resented as undemocratic. Or maybe its use in training dogs to retrieve has made some people feel that it is an undignified word to apply to human beings. But, whatever the reason, there is a growing uncertainty about its status, and hence it is the sort of word that conscientious people look up in a dictionary.

Will they find it labeled "good" or "bad"? Neither, of course, because either applied indiscriminately would be untrue. The Third International lists nineteen different meanings of the verb *to fetch.* Of these some are labeled "dialectal," some "chiefly dialectal," some "obsolete," one "chiefly Scottish," and two "not in formal use." The primary meaning— "to go after and bring back" —is not labeled and hence can be accepted as standard, accepted with the more assurance because the many shades of labeling show us that the word's status has been carefully considered.

On grammatical questions the Third International tries to be equally exact and thorough. Sometimes a construction is listed without comment, meaning that in the opinion of the editors it is unquestionably respectable. Sometimes a construction carries the comment "used by speakers and writers on all educational levels though disapproved by some grammarians." Or the comment may be "used in substandard speech and formerly also by reputable writers." Or "less often in standard than in substandard speech." Or simply "dial."

And this very accurate reporting is based on evidence which is presented for our examination. One may feel that the evidence is inadequate or that the evaluation of it is erroneous. But surely, in the face of classification so much more elaborate and careful than any known heretofore, one cannot fly into a rage and insist that the dictionary is "out to destroy . . . every vestige of linguistic punctilio . . . every criterion for distinguishing between better usages and worse."

Words, as we have said, are continually shifting their meanings and connotations and hence their status. A word which has dignity, say, in the vocabulary of an older person may go down in other people's estimation. Like *fetch*. The older speaker is not likely to be aware of this and will probably be inclined to ascribe the snickers of the young at his speech to that degeneration of manners which every generation has deplored in its juniors. But a word which is coming up in the scale—like *jazz*, say, or, more recently, *crap*—will strike his ear at once. We are much more aware of offenses given us than of those we give. And if he turns to a dictionary and finds the offending word listed as standard—or even listed, apparently—his response is likely to be an outburst of indignation.

But the dictionary can neither snicker nor fulminate. It records. It will offend many, no doubt, to find the expression *wise up*, meaning to inform or to become informed, listed in the Third International with no restricting label. To my aging ears it still sounds like slang. But the evidence—quotations from the *Kiplinger Washington Letter* and the *Wall Street Journal*—convinces me that it is I who am out of step, lagging behind. If such publications have taken to using *wise up* in serious contexts, with no punctuational indication of irregularity, then it is obviously respectable. And finding it so listed and supported, I can only say that it's nice to be informed and sigh to realize that I am becoming an old fogy. But, of course, I don't have to use it (and I'll be damned if I will! "Let them smile, as I do now, At the old forsaken bough Where I cling").

In part, the trouble is due to the fact that there is no standard for standard. Ideas of what is proper to use in serious, dignified speech and writing are changing—and with breathtaking rapidity. This is one of the major facts of contemporary American English. But it is no more the dictionary's business to oppose this process than to speed it up.

Even in our standard speech some words are more dignified

and some more informal than others, and dictionaries have tried
to guide us through these uncertainties by marking certain words
and constructions as "colloquial," meaning "inappropriate in a
formal situation." But this distinction, in the opinion of most
scholars, has done more harm than good. It has created the notion
that these particular words are inferior, when actually they might
be the best possible words in 'an informal statement. And so—to
the rage of many reviewers—the Third International has dropped
this label. Not all labels, as angrily charged, but only this one out
of a score. And the doing so may have been an error, but it certainly didn't constitute "betrayal" or "abandoning of all distinctions." It was intended to end a certain confusion.

In all the finer shades of meaning, of which the status of a word
is only one, the user is on his own, whether he likes it or not. Despite *Life's* artless assumption about the Gettysburg Address,
nothing worth writing is written *from* a dictionary. The dictionary,
rather, comes along afterwards and describes what *has been*
written.

Words in themselves are not dignified, or silly, or wise, or malicious. But they can be used in dignified, silly, wise, or malicious
ways by dignified, silly, wise, or malicious people. *Egghead,* for
example, is a perfectly legitimate word, as legitimate as *highbrow*
or *long-haired.* But there is something very wrong and very undignified, by civilized standards, in a belligerent dislike for intelligence and education. *Yak* is an amusing word for persistent
chatter. Anyone could say, "We were just yakking over a cup of
coffee," with no harm to his dignity. But to call a Supreme Court
decision *yakking* is to be vulgarly insulting and so, undignified.
Again, there's nothing wrong with *confab* when it's appropriate.
But when the work of a great research project, employing hundreds of distinguished scholars over several decades and involving the honor of one of the greatest publishing houses in the
world, is described as *confabbing* (as the New York *Times* editorially described the preparation of the Third International), the
use of this particular word asserts that the lexicographers had
merely sat around and talked idly. And the statement becomes
undignified—if not, indeed, slanderous.

The lack of dignity in such statements is not in the words, nor in
the dictionaries that list them, but in the hostility that deliberately

seeks this tone of expression. And in expressing itself the hostility frequently shows that those who are expressing it don't know how to use a dictionary. Most of the reviewers seem unable to read the Third International and unwilling to read the Second.

The *American Bar Association Journal,* for instance, in a typical outburst ("a deplorable abdication of responsibility"), picked out for special scorn the inclusion in the Third International of the word *irregardless.* "As far as the new Webster's is concerned," said the *Journal,* "this meaningless verbal bastard is just as legitimate as any other word in the dictionary." Thirty seconds spent in examining the book they were so roundly condemning would have shown them that in it *irregardless* is labeled "nonstand"—which means "nonstandard," which means "not conforming to the usage generally characteristic of educated native speakers of the language." Is that "just as legitimate as any other word in the dictionary"?

The most disturbing fact of all is that the editors of a dozen of the most influential publications in America today are under the impression that *authoritative* must mean *authoritarian.* Even the "permissive" Third International doesn't recognize this identification—editors' attitudes being not yet, fortunately, those of the American people. But the Fourth International may have to.

The new dictionary may have many faults. Nothing that tries to meet an ever-changing situation over a terrain as vast as contemporary English can hope to be free of them. And much in it is open to honest, and informed, disagreement. There can be linguistic objection to the eradication of proper names. The removal of guides to pronunciation from the foot of every page may not have been worth the valuable space it saved. The new method of defining words of many meanings has disadvantages as well as advantages. And of the half million or more definitions, hundreds, possibly thousands, may seem inadequate or imprecise. To some (of whom I am one) the omission of the label "colloquial" will seem meritorious; to others it will seem a loss.

But one thing is certain: anyone who solemnly announces in the year 1962 that he will be guided in matters of English usage by a dictionary published in 1934 is talking ignorant and pretentious nonsense.

DISCUSSION

Bergen Evans defends the new dictionary; how does the title
of his essay indicate his position? How does he turn his op-
ponents' arguments against them? Evans refers to the unhappi-
ness of the Washington *Post* with the new definition of "door";
why does he choose such a mundane, everyday object as a door
for his illustration? What does he do with the newspaper's objection? Is he effective? What do you think of his reference to
Dr. Johnson's famous definition? In this connection you might
compare your dictionary's definition to that of Dr. Johnson.

Try to define something commonplace like "bottle," "step,"
"floor," or "window."

What does Evans mean when he says the new edition's critics
confuse "authoritative" and "authoritarian"?

Webster's New Word Book

NORMAN E. ISAACS

A passel of double-domes at the G. & C. Merriam Company joint in Springfield, Mass., have been confabbing and yakking for twenty-seven years—which is not intended to infer that they have not been doing plenty work—and now they have finalized Webster's Third New International Dictionary, Unabridged, a new edition of that swell and esteemed word book.

Those who regard the foregoing paragraph as acceptable English prose will find that the new Webster's is just the dictionary for them. The words in that paragraph all are listed in the new work with no suggestion that they are anything but standard.

Webster's has, it is apparent, surrendered to the permissive school that has been busily extending its beachhead on English instruction in the schools. This development is disastrous because, intentionally or unintentionally, it serves to reinforce the notion that good English is whatever is popular. At a time when complaints are heard in many quarters that youths entering colleges and graduate schools are unequipped to use their mother tongue and that the art of clear communication has been impaired, the publication of a say-as-you-go dictionary can only accelerate the deterioration. Its appearance is bound to cause dismay among the sounder teachers, among publishers, among editors, among foreigners striving to learn our language—among all those who seek more in a dictionary than a mere mechanical registering of how Polly Adler, Art Linkletter and even bona fide writers use the language.

On the credit side, the editors have coped admirably with the lexical explosion that has showered us with so many new words in recent years; they have included 100,000 new words or new definitions. These are improvements, but they cannot outweigh the fundamental fault.

Webster's is more than just a publishing venture; for generations it has been so widely regarded as a peerless authority on American English as to become almost a public institution. Its editors therefore have to some degree a public responsibility. In issuing the Third New International they have not lived up to it. We suggest to the Webster editors that they not throw out the printing plates of the Second Edition. There is likely to be a continuing demand for it; and perhaps that edition can be made the platform for a new start—admittedly long, arduous and costly. But a new start is needed.

Keep Your Old Webster's

THE WASHINGTON POST

If your old copy of the unabridged second edition of *Webster's New International Dictionary of the English Language,* published in Springfield, Massachusetts, is battered and dog-eared, don't throw it away. If you love truth, accuracy, and a little grammar to improve your speech or writing, hang on to it. You are not likely to find its virtues in the new third edition which recently appeared. The lexicographical mountain labored—labored since 1936—and brought forth a monstrosity. The nature of the monstrosity is detailed in an indictment printed in the current *Atlantic Monthly* by Wilson Follett under the title, "Sabotage in Springfield." Mr. Follett, himself an authority on matters literary and linguistic, is apoplectic at the sins of commission and omission that he finds in the new edition. By no stretch of the imaginiation can the new volume supersede the excellent second edition, which has held a place of authority for many years.

Indeed, Mr. Follett and countless working editors regard as the worst sin of the new dictionary its complete abdication of authority. Anything goes: colloquialisms, slovenly diction, bad grammar, and barbarisms of all sorts if enough people seem to like them! It also omits the Gazetteer, the Biographical Dictionary, and the key to pronunciation found in the second edition at the bottom of facing pages. Mr. Follett laments that one cannot find in it the names of the apostles or the location of the District of Columbia.

The new dictionary illustrates one of the cardinal sins of learned communication in the present day: pretentious and obscure verbosity. Take, for instance, its definition of so simple an object as a door: "a movable piece of firm material or a structure supported usually along one side and swinging on pivots or hinges, sliding along a groove, rolling up and down, revolving as one of four leaves, or folding like an accordion by means of which an opening may be closed or kept open for passage into or out of a building, room, or other covered enclosure or a car, airplane, elevator, or other vehicle." Or look up the definition of *waltz*, which, we learn after many words, is "a constant gyrating motion," clearly a dance in the lexicographer's mind to wind up the twist. Accuracy and brevity, gentlemen of Springfield, are virtues too rashly abandoned nowadays. We ought at least to look for these in a dictionary.

Two Journals Score New Dictionary

FOSTER HAILEY

Two more voices have been added to the learned criticism that has been falling upon the editors of Webster's Third New International Dictionary of the English Language since its appearance last September.

A reviewer in *The Library Journal*, which has a wide circulation among librarians, said the editors had failed to make the new edition the yardstick of good usage that a dictionary should be.

"The great mass of dictionary users want and need a dictionary to prescribe for them," B. Hunter Smeaton of Los Angeles State College wrote. " 'Prescribe' not in the authoritarian sense or in that of any effort to arrest the perpetual change inherent in language, but in the sense of bold-facing those forms most widely acceptable in the current generation's custodians of preferred usage (ultimately teachers and editors)."

"It is no snobbery to ask for a yardstick to measure by,' he continued.

The January issue of *The American Bar Association Journal*, edited by Richard Bentley of Chicago, was also critical. In an editorial titled "Logomachy—Debased Verbal Currency," it said "a serious blow has recently befallen the cause of good English."

"The most serious indictment of the new dictionary," the editorial said, "is that it has utterly abdicated any role as judge of what is good English usage. We join in what seems to be a general feeling that this abdication of responsibility for the standards of language is deplorable."

Gresham's Law—that bad money drives out good—now seems to have been transferred to language, the editorial said.

5

The Language Exploited and Exploded and Occasionally Exuberated and Extravagated

THE FIRST THREE SELECTIONS in this section concern themselves with what language specialists call jargon, the language peculiar to a particular group or activity, and this may lead a reader to wonder why the fourth selection is in this section at all, a question to be dealt with later on.

We all speak jargon, willy-nilly; Professor Laird, in his essay in Chapter 2, pointed out how dialect is everywhere, and dialect precedes jargon. We speak in jargon when we discuss a sporting event—The scatback was a good broken-field runner. He was ahead thirty-love when a fault was called on him. With two up and two down, the count three and two, the veteran third-sacker parked a change-up pitch in the upper deck. Try to imagine what someone who knew nothing about baseball would do with the last sentence. Atomic physicists converse in jargon, as do auto mechanics and television repairmen, English teachers and college freshmen, which is only to say that we all use words in special senses in special situations, as a kind of verbal shorthand. The electrician says, "I'll have to run the ground through those studs." The truck driver says, "My rig skidded and jackknifed on that hairpin turn." The student says, "Do we need bluebooks for the final? Is it open-book?" Each is understood clearly if he speaks in the proper situation. Jargon, then, can be perfectly acceptable, even preferred, as can be illustrated by an attempt to revise any of the above to assure its clarity to any user of the language; try it. The following selections are not concerned with the kind of jargon we might term the technical or specialized language of some particular activity; the authors are concerned with what they see as the perversion of the language through a misuse of jargon, a failure to use it in the proper place or in the proper manner.

The first essay, by Stuart Chase, is an illustration in its title of how words can be coined. Congressman Maury Maverick, whose very name repeated an earlier coinage, first used the term "gobbledygook" when he became exasperated in his efforts to read and understand government publications. The term has stayed with us; how does your dictionary label it?

Gobbledygook

STUART CHASE

Said Franklin Roosevelt, in one of his early presidential speeches: "I see one-third of a nation ill-housed, ill-clad, ill-nourished." Translated into standard bureaucratic prose his statement would read:

It is evident that a substantial number of persons within the Continental boundaries of the United States have inadequate financial resources with which to purchase the products of agricultural communities and industrial establishments. It would appear that for a considerable segment of the population, possibly as much as 33.3333* of the total, there are inadequate housing facilities, and an equally significant proportion is deprived of the proper types of clothing and nutriment.

This rousing satire on gobbledygook—or talk among the bureaucrats—is adapted from a report[1] prepared by the Federal Security Agency in an attempt to break out of the verbal squirrel cage. "Gobbledygook" was coined by an exasperated Congressman, Maury Maverick of Texas, and means using two, or three, or ten words in the place of one, or using a five-syllable word where a single syllable would suffice. Maverick was censuring the forbidding prose of executive departments in Washington, but the term has now spread to windy and pretentious language in general.

"Gobbledygook" itself is a good example of the way a language grows. There was no word for the event before Maverick's invention; one had to say: "You know, that terrible, involved, polysyllabic language those government people use down in Washington." Now one word takes the place of a dozen.

*Not carried beyond four places.
[1]This and succeeding quotations from F.S.A. report by special permission of the author, Milton Hall.

A British member of Parliament, A. P. Herbert, also exasperated with bureaucratic jargon, translated Nelson's immortal phrase, "England expects every man to do his duty":

England anticipates that, as regards the current emergency, personnel will face up to the issues, and exercise appropriately the functions allocated to their respective occupational groups.

A New Zealand official made the following report after surveying a plot of ground for an athletic field:[2]

It is obvious from the difference in elevation with relation to the short depth of the property that the contour is such as to preclude any reasonable developmental potential for active recreation.

Seems the plot was too steep.

An office manager sent this memo to his chief:

Verbal contact with Mr. Blank regarding the attached notification of promotion has elicited the attached representation intimating that he prefers to decline the assignment.

Seems Mr. Blank didn't want the job.

A doctor testified at an English trial that one of the parties was suffering from "circumorbital haematoma."

Seems the party had a black eye.

In August 1952 the U.S. Department of Agriculture put out a pamphlet entitled: "Cultural and Pathogenic Variability in Single-Condial and Hyphaltip Isolates of Hemlin-Thosporium Turcicum Pass."

Seems it was about corn leaf disease.

On reaching the top of the Finsteraarhorn in 1845, M. Dollfus-Ausset, when he got his breath, exclaimed:

The soul communes in the infinite with those icy peaks which seem to have their roots in the bowels of eternity.

Seems he enjoyed the view.

[2]This item and the next two are from the piece on gobbledygook by W. E. Farbstein, *New York Times*, March 29, 1953.

A government department announced:

Voucherable expenditures necessary to provide adequate dental treatment required as adjunct to medical treatment being rendered a pay patient in in-patient status may be incurred as required at the expense of the Public Health Service.

Seems you can charge your dentist bill to the Public Health Service. Or can you?

LEGAL TALK   Gobbledygook not only flourishes in government bureaus but grows wild and lush in the law, the universities, and sometimes among the literati. Mr. Micawber was a master of gobbledygook, which he hoped would improve his fortunes. It is almost always found in offices too big for face-to-face talk. Gobbledygook can be defined as squandering words, packing a message with excess baggage and so introducing semantic "noise." Or it can be scrambling words in a message so that meaning does not come through. The directions on cans, bottles, and packages for putting the contents to use are often a good illustration. Gobbledygook must not be confused with double talk, however, for the intentions of the sender are usually honest.

I offer you a round fruit and say, "Have an orange." Not so an expert in legal phraseology, as parodied by editors of *Labor:*

I hereby give and convey to you, all and singular, my estate and interests, right, title, claim and advantages of and in said orange, together with all rind, juice, pulp and pits, and all rights and advantages therein . . . anything hereinbefore or hereinafter or in any other deed or deeds, instrument or instruments of whatever nature or kind whatsoever, to the contrary, in any wise, notwithstanding.

The state of Ohio, after five years of work, has redrafted its legal code in modern English, eliminating 4,500 sections and doubtless a blizzard of "whereases" and "hereinafters." Legal terms of necessity must be closely tied to their referents, but the early solons tried to do this the hard way, by adding synonyms. They hoped to trap the physical event in a net of words, but instead they created a mumbo-jumbo beyond the power of the layman, and even many a lawyer, to translate. Legal talk is studded with tautologies, such as "cease and desist," "give and convey," "irrelevant, incompetent, and immaterial." Furthermore, legal jargon is a dead language; it is not spoken and it is not growing. An official of one of the big insurance companies calls their branch of it "bafflegab." Here is a sample from his collection:[3]

One-half to his mother, if living, if not to his father, and one-half to his mother-in-law, if living, if not to his mother, if living, if not to his father. Thereafter payment is to be made in a single sum to his brothers. On the one-half payable to his mother, if living, if not to his father, he does not bring in his mother-in-law as the next payee to receive, although on the one-half to his mother-in-law, he does bring in the mother or father.

You apply for an insurance policy, pass the tests, and instead of a straightforward "here is your policy," you receive something like this:

This policy is issued in consideration of the application therefor, copy of which application is attached hereto and made part hereof, and of the payment for said insurance on the life of the above-named insured.

ACADEMIC TALK   The pedagogues may be less repetitious than the lawyers, but many use even longer words. It is a symbol of their calling to prefer Greek and Latin derivatives to Anglo-Saxon. Thus instead of saying: "I like short clear words," many a professor would think it more seemly to say: "I prefer an abbreviated phraseology, distinguished for its lucidity." Your professor is sometimes right, the longer word may carry the meaning better— but not because it is long. Allen Upward in his book *The New Word* warmly advocates Anglo-Saxon English as against what he calls "Mediterranean" English, with its polysyllables built up like a skyscraper.

Professional pedagogy, still alternating between the Middle Ages and modern science, can produce what Henshaw Ward once called the most repellent prose known to man. It takes an iron will to read as much as a page of it. Here is a sample of what is known in some quarters as "pedageese":

[3]Interview with Clifford B. Reeves by Sylvia F. Porter, *New York Evening Post*, March 14, 1952.

Realization has grown that the curriculum or the experiences of learners change and improve only as those who are most directly involved examine their goals, improve their understandings and increase their skill in performing the tasks necessary to reach newly defined goals. This places the focus upon teacher, lay citizen and learner as partners in curricular improvement and as the individuals who must change, if there is to be curriculum change.

I think there is an idea concealed here somewhere. I think it means: "If we are going to change the curriculum, teacher, parent, and student must all help." The reader is invited to get out his semantic decoder and check on my translation. Observe there is no technical language in this gem of pedageese, beyond possibly the word "curriculum." It is just a simple idea heavily ververbalized.

In another kind of academic talk the author may display his learning to conceal a lack of ideas. A bright instructor, for instance, in need of prestige may select a common sense proposition for the subject of a learned monograph—say, "Modern cities are hard to live in" and adorn it with imposing polysyllables: "Urban existence in the perpendicular declivities of megalopolis . . ." et cetera. He coins some new terms to transfix the reader—"megadecibel" or "strato-cosmopolis"—and works them vigorously. He is careful to add a page or two of differential equations to show the "scatter." And then he publishes, with 147 footnotes and a bibliography to knock your eye out. If the authorities are dozing, it can be worth an associate professorship.

While we are on campus, however, we must not forget that the technical language of the natural sciences and some terms in the social sciences, forbidding as they may sound to the layman, are quite necessary. Without them, specialists could not communicate what they find. Trouble arises when experts expect the uninitiated to understand the words; when they tell the jury, for instance, that the defendant is suffering from "circumorbital haematoma."

Here are two authentic quotations. Which was written by a distinguished modern author, and which by a patient in a mental hospital? You will find the answer at the end of this essay.

(1) Have just been to supper. Did not knowing what the woodchuck

sent me here. How when the blue blue blue on the said anyone can do it that tries. Such is the presidential candidate.

(2) No history of a family to close with those and close. Never shall he be alone to be alone to be alone to be alone to be alone to lend a hand and leave it left and wasted.

REDUCING THE GOBBLE   As government and business offices grow larger, the need for doing something about gobbledygook increases. Fortunately the biggest office in the world is working hard to reduce it. The Federal Security Agency in Washington,[4] with nearly 100 million clients on its books, began analyzing its communication lines some years ago, with gratifying results. Surveys find trouble in three main areas: correspondence with clients about their social security problems, office memos, official reports.

Clarity and brevity, as well as common humanity, are urgently needed in this vast establishment which deals with disability, old age, and unemployment. The surveys found instead many cases of long-windedness, foggy meanings, clichés, and singsong phrases, and gross neglect of the reader's point of view. Rather than talking to a real person, the writer was talking to himself. "We often write like a man walking on stilts."

Here is a typical case of long-windedness:

Gobbledygook as found: "We are wondering if sufficient time has passed so that you are in a position to indicate whether favorable action may now be taken on our recommendation for the reclassification of Mrs. Blank, junior clerk-stenographer, CAF 2, to assistant clerk-stenographer, CAF 3?"

Suggested improvement: "Have you yet been able to act on our recommendation to reclassify Mrs. Blank?"

Another case:

Although the Central Efficiency Rating Committee recognizes that there are many desirable changes that could be made in the present efficiency rating system in order to make it more realistic and more workable than it now is, this committee is of the opinion that no further change should be made in the present system during the

[4]Now the Department of Health, Education, and Welfare.

current year. Because of conditions prevailing throughout the country and the resultant turnover in personnel, and difficulty in administering the Federal programs, further mechanical improvement in the present rating system would require staff retraining and other administrative expense which would seem best withheld until the official termination of hostilities, and until restoration of regular operations.

The F.S.A. invites us to squeeze the gobbledygook out of this statement. Here is my attempt:

The Central Efficiency Rating Committee recognizes that desirable changes could be made in the present system. We believe, however, that no change should be attempted until the war is over.

This cuts the statement from 111 to 30 words, about one-quarter of the original, but perhaps the reader can do still better. What of importance have I left out?

Sometimes in a book which I am reading for information—not for literary pleasure—I run a pencil through the surplus words. Often I can cut a section to half its length with an improvement in clarity. Magazines like *The Reader's Digest* have reduced this process to an art. Are long-windedness and obscurity a cultural lag from the days when writing was reserved for priests and cloistered scholars? The more words and the deeper the mystery, the greater their prestige and the firmer the hold on their jobs. And the better the candidate's chance today to have his doctoral thesis accepted.

The F.S.A. surveys found that a great deal of writing was obscure although not necessarily prolix. Here is a letter sent to more than 100,000 inquirers, a classic example of murky prose. To clarify it, one needs to *add* words, not cut them:

In order to be fully insured, an individual must have earned $50 or more in covered employment for as many quarters of coverage as half the calendar quarters elapsing between 1936 and the quarter in which he reaches age 65 or dies, whichever first occurs.

Probably no one without the technical jargon of the office could translate this: nevertheless, it was sent out to drive clients mad for seven years. One poor fellow wrote back: "I am no longer in covered employment. I have an outside job now."

Many words and phrases in officialese seem to come out automatically, as if from lower centers of the brain. In this standardized prose people never *get jobs,* they "secure employment"; *before* and *after* become "prior to" and "subsequent to"; one does not *do,* one "performs"; nobody *knows* a thing, he is "fully cognizant"; one never *says,* he "indicates." A great favorite at present is "implement."

Some charming boners occur in this talking-in-one's-sleep. For instance:

The problem of extending coverage to all employees, regardless of size, is not as simple as surface appearances indicate.

Though the proportions of all males and females in ages 16–45 are essentially the same . . .

Dairy cattle, usually and commonly embraced in dairying . . .

In its manual to employees, the F.S.A. suggests the following:

Instead of	Use
give consideration to	consider
make inquiry regarding	inquire
is of the opinion	believes
comes into conflict with	conflicts
information which is of a	confidential
confidential nature	information

Professional or office gobbledygook often arises from using the passive rather than the active voice. Instead of looking you in the eye, as it were, and writing "This act requires . . ." the office worker looks out of the window and writes: "It is required by this statute that . . ." When the bureau chief says, "We expect Congress to cut your budget," the message is only too clear; but usually he says, "It is expected that the departmental budget estimates will be reduced by Congress."

Gobbled: "All letters prepared for the signature of the Administrator will be single spaced."

Ungobbled: "Single space all letters for the Administrator." (Thus cutting 13 words to 7.)

ONLY PEOPLE CAN READ   The F.S.A. surveys pick up the point that human communication involves a listener as well as a speaker. Only people can read, though a lot of writing seems to be addressed to beings in outer space. To whom are you talking? The sender of the officialese message often forgets the chap on the other end of the line.

A woman with two small children wrote the F.S.A. asking what she should do about payments, as her husband had lost his memory. "If he never gets able to work," she said, "and stays in an institution would I be able to draw any benefits? . . . I don't know how I am going to live and raise my children since he is disable to work. Please give me some information. . . ."

To this human appeal, she received a shattering blast of gobbledygook, beginning, "State unemployment compensation laws do not provide any benefits for sick or disabled individuals . . . in order to qualify an individual must have a certain number of quarters of coverage . . ." et cetera, et cetera. Certainly if the writer had been thinking about the poor woman he would not have dragged in unessential material about old-age insurance. If he had pictured a mother without means to care for her children, he would have told her where she might get help—from the local office which handles aid to dependent children, for instance.

Gobbledygook of this kind would largely evaporate if we thought of our messages as two way—in the above case, if we pictured ourselves talking on the doorstep of a shabby house to a woman with two children tugging at her skirts, who in her distress does not know which way to turn.

RESULTS OF THE SURVEY   The F.S.A. survey showed that office documents could be cut 20 to 50 per cent, with an improvement in clarity and a great saving to taxpayers in paper and payrolls.

A handbook was prepared and distributed to key officials.[5] They read it, thought about it, and presently began calling section meetings to discuss gobbledygook. More booklets were ordered, and the local output of documents began to improve. A Correspondence Review Section was established as a kind of laboratory to

[5] By Milton Hall.

test murky messages. A supervisor could send up samples for analysis and suggestions. The handbook is now used for training new members; and many employees keep it on their desks along with the dictionary. Outside the Bureau some 25,000 copies have been sold (at 20 cents each) to individuals, governments, business firms, all over the world. It is now used officially in the Veterans Administration and in the Department of Agriculture.

The handbook makes clear the enormous amount of gobbledygook which automatically spreads in any large office, together with ways and means to keep it under control. I would guess that at least half of all the words circulating around the bureaus of the world are "irrelevant, incompetent, and immaterial"—to use a favorite legalism; or just plain "unnecessary"—to ungobble it.

My favorite story of removing the gobble from gobbledygook concerns the Bureau of Standards at Washington. I have told it before but perhaps the reader will forgive the repetition. A New York plumber wrote the Bureau that he had found hydrochloric acid fine for cleaning drains, and was it harmless? Washington replied: "The efficacy of hydrochloric acid is indisputable, but the chlorine residue is incompatible with metallic permanence."

The plumber wrote back that he was mighty glad the Bureau agreed with him. The Bureau replied with a note of alarm: "We cannot assume responsibility for the production of toxic and noxious residues with hydrochloric acid, and suggest that you use an alternate procedure." The plumber was happy to learn that the Bureau still agreed with him.

Whereupon Washington exploded: "Don't use hydrochloric acid; it eats hell out of the pipes!"

Note: The second quotation on page 103 comes from Gertrude Stein's *Lucy Church Amiably.*

DISCUSSION

What does your dictionary say about "gobbledygook"? What usage level is assigned to it? What speculations can you make about its source? Does it appear that Congressman Maverick just made it up?

Mr. Chase is arguing for writing that communicates; note his emphasis upon the audience; note also that he does not deny the use of a specialized language, only arguing that specialized language does not communicate when directed to readers who are not specialists. Chase really attacks two kinds of language misuse, then; one is mentioned above, the use of specialized language in inappropriate circumstances (the doctor and his "circumorbital haematoma"), and the second object of his ire is language that is complicated and involved for no real reason whatever, as in the response received by the plumber. Look for examples of each kind of language misuse. Texts, college catalogues and bulletins, announcements, magazines, and newspapers will provide many examples. Look for examples of specialized language used properly and improperly and examples of pure gobbledygook or bafflegab.

How to Write Like a Social Scientist

SAMUEL T. WILLIAMSON

During my years as an editor I have seen probably hundreds of job applicants who were either just out of college or in their senior years. All wanted "to write." Many brought letters from their teachers. But I do not recall one letter announcing that its bearer could write what he wished to say with clarity and directness, with economy of words, and with pleasing variety of sentence structure.

Most of these young men and women could not write plain English. Apparently their noses had not been rubbed in the drudgery of putting one simple, well-chosen word behind the other. If this was true of teachers' pets, what about the rest? What about those going into business and industry? Or those going into professions? What about those who remain at college—first for a Master of Arts degree, then an instructorship combined with work for a Ph.D., then perhaps an assistant professorship, next a full professorship and finally, as an academic crown of laurel, appointment as head of a department or as dean of a faculty?

Certainly, faculty members of a front-rank university should be better able to express themselves than those they teach. Assume that those in the English department have this ability: Can the same be said of the social scientists—economists, sociologists, and authorities on government? We need today as we never needed so urgently before all the understanding they can give us of problems of earning a living, caring for our fellows, and governing ourselves. Too many of them, I find, can't write as well as their students.

I am still convalescing from overexposure some time ago to

products of the academic mind. One of the foundations engaged me to edit the manuscripts of a socio-economic research report designed for the thoughtful citizen as well as for the specialist. My expectations were not high—no deathless prose, merely a sturdy, no-nonsense report of explorers into the wilderness of statistics and half-known fact. I knew from experience that economic necessity compels many a professional writer to be a cream skimmer and a gatherer of easily obtainable material; for unless his publisher will stand the extra cost, he cannot afford the exhaustive investigation which endowed research makes possible. Although I did not expect fine writing from a trained, professional researcher, I did assume that a careful fact-finder would write carefully.

And so, anticipating no literary treat, I plunged into the forest of words of my first manuscript. My weapons were a sturdy eraser and several batteries of sharpened pencils. My armor was a thesaurus. And if I should become lost, a near-by public library was a landmark, and the Encyclopedia of Social Sciences on its reference shelves was an ever-ready guide.

Instead of big trees, I found underbrush. Cutting through involved, lumbering sentences was bad enough, but the real chore was removal of the burdocks of excess verbiage which clung to the manuscript. Nothing was big or large; in my author's lexicon, it was "substantial." When he meant "much" he wrote "to a substantially high degree." If some event took place in the early 1920's he put it "in the early part of the decade of the twenties." And instead of "that depends," my author wrote, "any answer to this question must bear in mind certain peculiar characteristics of the industry."

So it went for 30,000 words. The pile of verbal burdocks grew—sometimes twelve words from a twenty-word sentence. The shortened version of 20,000 words was perhaps no more thrilling than the original report; but it was terser and crisper. It took less time to read and it could be understood quicker. That was all I could do. As S. S. McClure once said to me, "An editor can improve a manuscript, but he cannot put in what isn't there."

I did not know the author I was editing; after what I did to his copy, it may be just as well that we have not met. Aside from his cat-chasing-its-own-tail verbosity, he was a competent enough workman. Apparently he is well thought of. He has his doctorate, he is a trained researcher and a pupil of an eminent professor. He has held a number of fellowships and he has performed competently several jobs of economic research. But, after this long academic preparation for what was to be a life work, it is a mystery why so little attention was given to acquiring use of simple English.

Later, when I encountered other manuscripts, I found I had been too hard on this promising PhD. Tone-deaf as he was to words, his report was a lighthouse of clarity among the chapters turned in by his so-called academic betters. These brethern—and sister'n—who contributed the remainder of the foundation's study were professors and assistant professors in our foremost colleges and universities. The names of one or two are occasionally in newspaper headlines. All of them had, as the professorial term has it, "published."

Anyone who edits copy, regardless of whether it is good or bad, discovers in a manuscript certain pet phrases, little quirks of style and other individual traits of its author. But in the series I edited, all twenty reports read alike. Their words would be found in any English dictionary, grammar was beyond criticism, but long passages in these reports demanded not editing but actual translation. For hours at a time, I floundered in brier patches like this: "In eliminating wage changes due to purely transitory conditions, collective bargaining has eliminated one of the important causes of industrial conflict, for changes under such conditions are almost always followed by a reaction when normal conditions appear."

I am not picking on my little group of social scientists. They are merely members of a caste; they are so used to taking in each other's literary washing that it has become a habit for them to clothe their thoughts in the same smothering verbal garments. Nor are they any worse than most of their colleagues, for example:

In the long run, developments in transportation, housing, optimum size of plant, etc., might tend to induce an industrial and demographic pattern similar to the one that consciousness of vulnerability would dictate. Such a tendency might be advanced by public persuasion and governmental inducement, and advanced more effectively if the causes of urbanization had been carefully studied.

Such pedantic Choctaw may be all right as a sort of code language or shorthand of social science to circulate among initiates, but its perpetrators have no right to impose it on others. The tragedy is that its users appear to be under the impression that it is good English usage.

Father, forgive them; for they know not what they do! There once was a time when everyday folk spoke one language, and learned men wrote another. It was called the Dark Ages. The world is in such a state that we may return to the Dark Ages if we do not acquire wisdom. If social scientists have answers to our problems yet feel under no obligation to make themselves understood, then we laymen must learn their language. This may take some practice, but practice should become perfect by following six simple rules of the guild of social science writers. Examples which I give are sound and well tested; they come from manuscripts I edited.

RULE 1. *Never use a short word when you can think of a long one.* Never say "now" but "currently." It is not "soon" but "presently." You did not have "enough" but a "sufficiency." Never do you come to the "end" but to the "termination." This rule is basic.

RULE 2. *Never use one word when you can use two or more.* Eschew "probably." Write, "it is probable," and raise this to "it is not improbable." Then you'll be able to parlay "probably" into "available evidence would tend to indicate that it is not unreasonable to suppose."

RULE 3. *Put one-syllable thought into polysyllabic terms.* Instead of observing that a work force might be bigger and better, write, "In addition to quantitative enlargement, it is not improbable that there is need also for qualitative improvement in the personnel of the service." If you have discovered that musicians out of practice can't hold jobs, report that "the fact of rapid deterioration of musical skill when not in use soon converts the employed into the unemployable." Resist the impulse to say that much men's clothing is machine made. Put it thus: "Nearly all operations in the industry lend themselves to performance by machine, and all grades of men's clothing sold in significant quantity involve a very substantial amount of machine work."

RULE 4. *Put the obvious in terms of the unintelligible.* When you write that "the product of the activity of janitors is expended in the identical locality in which that activity takes place," your lay reader is in for a time of it. After an hour's puzzlement, he may conclude that janitors' sweepings are thrown on the town dump. See what you can do with this: "Each article sent to the cleaner is handled separately." You become a member of the guild in good standing if you put it like this: "Within the cleaning plant proper the business of the industry involves several well-defined processes, which, from the economic point of view, may be characterized simply by saying that most of them require separate handling of each individual garment or piece of material to be cleaned."

RULE 5. *Announce what you are going to say before you say it.* This pitcher's wind-up technique before hurling towards—not at—home plate has two varieties. First is the quick wind-up: "In the following sections the policies of the administration will be considered." Then you become strong enough for the contortionist wind-up: "Perhaps more important, therefore, than the question of what standards are in a particular case, there are the questions of the extent of observance of these standards and the methods of their enforcement." Also, you can play with reversing Rule 5 and *say what you have said after you have said it.*

RULE 6. *Defend your style as "scientific."* Look down on—not up to—clear, simple English. Sneer at it as "popular." Scorn it as "journalistic." Explain your failure to put more mental sweat into your writing on the ground that "the social scientists who want to be scientific believe that we can have scientific description of human behavior and trustworthy predictions in the scientific sense only as we build adequate taxonomic systems for observable phenomena and symbolic systems for the manipulation of ideal and abstract entities."

For this explanation I am indebted to Lyman Bryson in an *SRL* article (Oct. 13, 1945) "Writers: Enemies of Social Science." Standing on ground considerably of his own choosing, Mr. Bryson argued against judging social science writing by literary standards.

Social scientists are not criticized because they are not literary artists. The trouble with social science does not lie in its special vocabulary. Those words are doubtless chosen with great care. The trouble is that too few social scientists take enough care with words outside their special vocabularies.

It is not too much to expect that teachers should be more competent in the art of explanation than those they teach. Teachers of social sciences diligently try to acquire knowledge; too few of them exert themselves enough to impart it intelligently.

Too long has this been excused as "the academic mind." It should be called by what it is: intellectual laziness and grubbyminded-ness.

DISCUSSION

Mr. Williamson takes the complaint registered by Stuart Chase and applies it to a particular activity. The essence of his comment lies in the opening sentence of the third paragraph, "Certainly, faculty members of a front-rank university should be better able to express themselves than those they teach." The next sentence presents an assumption, one you may question, and the third particularizes the observation for the purpose of Williamson's essay, narrowing the subject of effective use of language down to its application to one branch of learning, socal science.

After introducing his subject, Williamson begins his discussion of his experience with the social scientist's book with two paragraphs heavy with figurative language, presenting his experience metaphorically, likening it to working through a heavy forest. In the "Father, forgive them" paragraph he introduces a new point. Heretofore he has been assailing the social scientists for their ineffective use of language; in this paragraph he points out a possible danger of the failure to communicate effectively. He tells us that our world is in a perilous condition; hence, if the social scientists have some solution to the world's problems it is important that we be able to read and understand what they have to offer. But going on in this paragraph we see that apparently Mr. Williamson has given up, for he does not say that the social scientists must learn to write so we can understand them but that we will just have to learn to read their writing. Do you agree?

In order to help us understand the social scientists Williamson presents six rules. Is he being ironic?

Can You Understand the Rules of Federal Prose?

JAMES R. MASTERSON
and WENDELL BROOKS PHILLIPS

Unfortunately there are those who respond to the spirit but who have no capacity for the unremitting labor of emmets and beavers. Such persons may as well withdraw at this point and devote themselves to the writing of minor poems.

Strictly speaking, the rules of Federal Prose may best be derived by pure induction. After examining several million cubic feet of Federal writings, even the comparatively obtuse reader will eventually understand the principles which they exhibit. But this book is addressed to beginners who have not had the privilege of such perusal. For them the following rules will serve both as a test of innate capacity and, should the ultimate goal of Federal employment be reached, as a preliminary guide for composition:

(1) Use nouns in preference to verbs. Children, illiterates, and artists use verbs in abundance. But verbs are too direct, too outspoken, too naive, not abstract enough to suit the needs of Federal Prose. When you are absolutely obliged to use a verb, use if possible some form of "to be," or a verb ending in "-ize," "-ate" or "-ect."

ENGLISH	FEDERAL PROSE
Time flies.	Time is fugitive. Fugacity is characteristic of time.
Hens lay eggs.	Egg-laying characterizes hens. Hens are typically oviparous. Hens ovulate, though not continuously and not without exception. Gallinaceous ovulation is effected only by hens.

ENGLISH	FEDERAL PROSE
Jack fell down and broke his crown.	A youth designated only as "Jack" sustained, incident to a loss of equilibrium, a fracture of the cranium.
When the cat's away the mice will play.	Rodents, in the absence of their feline enemy, are prone to divert themselves.
Haste makes waste.	Precipitation entails negation of economy.
Every dog has his day.	In every canine lifespan is manifested a period of optimum euphoria.
Yours of the 20th received and contents noted.	Receipt by this office of your communication dated November 20, 1945, and cognizance of the contents thereof, are herewith acknowledged.
Please return these papers.	Return of papers is requested.
The old gray mare came out of the wilderness forty–fifty years ago.	At a period subsequent to 1905 but prior to 1915 the subject mare, described as anile and in consequence grizzled, issued for motives unknown from a region defined only as uninhabited.
Man proposes but God disposes.	Human planning is subject to divine controls.

(2) Use abstract and general nouns, not concrete and particular nouns. In other words, intellectualize your nominalism. Untutored minds see particular objects. Minds trained in the Federal service see patterns and essences illustrated in particular objects.

ENGLISH	FEDERAL PROSE
Roses are red.	Rosacae exhibit roseateness.
Scissors cut.	Scissors effect scission functionally.
Two heads are better than one.	Dual is preferred to unilateral consideration.

ENGLISH

FEDERAL PROSE

Call not thy brother "fool."

Avoid attribution of imbecility to your male sib.

The sun rises in the east.

Solar bodies tend to exhibit, with respect to and from the viewpoint of their satellites, an apparent orientality of anabasis.

Show your pass.

The display of your entrance permit is mandatory.

Hark! Hark! The dogs do bark.
　The beggars are coming to town—
Some in rags, and some in tags,
　And some in velvet gowns.

The canine ululations now obtrusively perceptible adumbrate the visitation cityward of mendicants exhibiting a variability of costume between the extremes of quasi-nudity and velours. Public protests have been received with respect to the imminent concentration of artists, convicts, and doctors of philosophy in the District of Columbia.

Satisfaction guaranteed or your money back.

The remittance of sums paid by customers purchasing articles in or of this establishment is hereby guaranteed in the event that such articles, or one or more thereof, shall be hereafter deemed unsatisfactory to or by the said customers, or any of them:—provided, however, (a) that the dissatisfaction be expressed verbally or through correspondence and not otherwise, (b) that the said dissatisfaction be expressed by a customer or customers, (c) that the said customer or customers be, or have been, customers of the establishment designated herein-above, and (d) that the said dissatisfaction relate to, and be justifiably directed toward, an article or articles purchased thereby herein.

ENGLISH	FEDERAL PROSE

Hey diddle diddle!
The cat and the fiddle!
    The cow jumped over the
    moon.
The little dog laughed
To see the sport,
    And the dish ran off with the
    spoon.
	The alarming because unprecedented spectacle of feline musicianship exhibited by means of catgut elicited from the spectators such reactions as, in the case of a cow, translunary saltation; of a diminutive canine, cachinnation; and of two articles of tableware, collusive flight.

(3) Use attributive nouns in preference to adjectives or adjectival phrases.

ENGLISH	FEDERAL PROSE
The writing of books is a trade.	Book composition is a trade.
The Department of the Interior.	The Interior Department.
The search for truth is endless.	The truthquest is interminable.

(4) Avoid the rigid and unnatural parallelism of English.

ENGLISH	FEDERAL PROSE
The candidate is not only young but pretty.	The candidate not only is youthful but also personable. The candidate is not juvenile merely but is personable as well. Not only juvenile, also the candidate is personable.
The candidate is neither young nor pretty.	The candidate neither is youthful or is she personable.
The market will go either up or down.	In the event of its instability the market either will ascend or descend.
A candidate is wanted who can read and write.	A candidate able to read and who can write is indicated.

(5) Place clauses and phrases in such a way as to hold attention.

ENGLISH	FEDERAL PROSE
My father died when I was a baby.	When an infant my father died.
While being examined the candidate went to sleep.	In the course of examination somnolence acquired complete mastery over the candidate.
One rule is bad; two are worse.	One rule is bad, two worse.

ENGLISH	FEDERAL PROSE
Finding no weapon on Jones, the police let him go.	Finding no weapon on him, Jones was released by the police.
The chairman finds that the third report duplicated the second.	It is ascertained by the chairman the tertiary report to be duplicated by the second.

(6) Indicate explicitly the relations among all facts and ideas that you express. Do not expect your reader to solve riddles. Leave nothing to his imagination, because (a) he probably has none or (b) he may imagine something erotic. Few Federal adults can interpret the following:

> Hickory, dickory, dock.
> A mouse ran up the clock.
> The princess hopped, the fiddlers stopped,
> Not knowing what to do.

Expand this approximately as follows:

A sound suggestive of but distinguishable from striking issued from a tall clock in a ballroom in which a princess was but the most distingushed of the gay multitude that whirled in unison to the strains of a corps of violinists. Startled by the sudden and discordant plangency, the beauteous scion of royalty stumbled to an abrupt halt in her graceful evolutions; the orchestra, confused by this cessation of movement, subsided into silence; and only after investigation had divulged the origin of the perturbing phenomena in the hitherto unsuspected ascent, within the clock, of a rodent that had in some manner not ascertained effected adit thereto, were the festivities resumed.

Figurative language (unless two or more figures are combined) is inappropriate to the Federal service. The following proverb would not be readily understood:

Though thou shouldest bray a fool in a mortar among wheat with a pestle, yet will not his foolishness depart from him.

This could be rewritten for Federal purposes somewhat as follows:

All efforts looking toward alteration induced from without of the congenital mental configuration of personnel are ill advised, adaptation of administrative methodology thereto in contradistinction to adaptation thereof of administrative methodology being indicated.

(7) When using words that are in dictionaries, use them in senses that are unknown to lexicographers. Employ either *synecdoche* (designation of part as whole or of whole as part) or *transference* (migration of meaning from a word to another word often found in the same context).

Classified documents: i.e., documents classified as restricted, confidential, secret, or top secret. (Non-Federal readers, coming upon this phrase, will suppose that it refers to documents that are arranged by a system of classification, as distinguished from documents not so arranged. In view of the nature of classified documents, it is well that they should be designated somewhat mysteriously, so that the general public will think that it knows what it does not know. If it knew that it cannot see the documents, it would want to see them.)

Document file: i.e., a file consisting of folded papers as distinguished from one consisting of flat or bound papers. (Here, again, non-Federal readers will suppose that they know what they do not know. They will assume that a document file is a file consisting of documents, as distinguished from a file consisting of something that is not documents. Not knowing that other files also consist of documents, they will not care to see those files.)

Higher or lower *echelons* of command. (Formerly, echelons were units of a body of troops, each, except the last, drawn up parallel to but to right or left of the unit in its rear. All the units were characterized by being at different distances from the officer in command. Levels of command in the hierarchy of army organization had the same characteristic. The mathematical line extending from an officer to an echelon is horizontal; the metaphysical line extending from an officer to his superior or subordinate is vertical; the two lines are at right angles to each other, forming a Greek cross of which the orientation is inconsequential and, if insisted on, would occasion intellectual strain.)

Inhabitants *evacuated* from a town. (Etymologically, to evacuate is to cause to be vacant or empty. A town is evacuated when it is caused to be vacant. Its inhabitants are evacuated when they are caused to be empty, as by catharsis or fright. The inhabitants can evacuate the town by leaving it. Military authorities can evacuate the town either by departing from it themselves or by causing the inhabitants to depart from it. In the latter event, the inhabitants are removed from the town. The removal of the inhabitants is equated with the evacuation of the town. Therefore evacuation is the same as removal. Therefore the inhabitants are evacuated from the town and are designated as evacuees.)

(8) Learn to punctuate scientifically.

a. Federal prose is not subject to the trivial rules of English punctuation, which were designed by pedants for the needless discomfiture of the young. The concepts of punctuation in Federal Prose are larger and broader than those entertained by novelists, poets, and scholars. . . .

b. When tempted to punctuate, first ask "Is it necessary?" Though use of a period at the end of a sentence is often allowable, even this can generally be avoided by a skillful grouping into sections, subsections, and sub-subsections, each with its proper symbol of designation and with the required degree of indentation.

c. Never use commas recklessly. The attempt to make a sentence clear on first reading is a juvenile practice that should be avoided.

ENGLISH	FEDERAL PROSE
Tom, Dick, and Harry went down the street.	Tom, Dick and Harry went down the street. (It is unnecessary to inquire whether the three persons mentioned went down the street, or whether Tom is being told that the other two did so. Even teachers and journalists are discarding use of the comma between the last two members of a series—and to this extent, English and Federal Prose are becoming ONE.)
The superintendent ordered the children to burn all waste paper, and teachers saw that the order was carried out.	The superintendent ordered the children to burn all waste paper and teachers saw that the order was carried out. (A comma in this sentence would insult the reader's intelligence.)

d. Use semicolons only under extreme duress. Any person whose thought-pattern includes the semicolon is not qualified to write Federal Prose. Typists are cautioned, however, not to remove this symbol from their machines (though the type-bar could be utilized for some more serviceable mark), since a few old-fashioned office chiefs insist on using semicolons in their letters to Congressmen.

e. The colon, on the other hand, is indispensable in Federal Prose, since it has become the great symbol of anticipation and logical order. There is, indeed, some question whether the Federal Government could operate without it. Skillfully used, it reveals the master, particularly in breaking the backbone of a stubborn sentence. Amateurish: "His favorite colors were red, green, and blue." Competent: "His favorite colors were: red, green and blue." Professional:

His favorite colors were:
  I. red
  II. green
  III. blue
  IV. or, a combination of the three above colors, with:
    A. red predominating
    B. green predominating
    C. blue predominating
    D. or, a balanced combination of the foregoing colors in which none of the following predominates:
        (x) red
        (y) green
        (z) blue

DISCUSSION

Do you understand how to write federal prose after reading Masterson and Phillips? Whereas Williamson criticized gobble-dygook as it appears in the writings of social scientists, Masterson and Phillips criticize it as it appears in what they term federal prose. Like Williamson, they offer rules for understanding a particular cant; also like Williamson, they often have their tongues in their cheeks. Note the form they adopt in their second paragraph. Ostensibly they are telling us how to write federal prose, that is, how to write gobbledygook. This is a device, a somewhat ironic one, for obviously they do not really intend to encourage anyone to write in the style of the examples they present. There is broad irony all through the essay; note the second rule, with its "intellectualize your nominalism." Can you figure out what the expression means from the context? Why do you suppose the authors used it?

Note the irony in the paragraph on evacuation; what is its effect here? The comment in 8c is downright savage, the parenthetical remark after "The superintendent ordered" very broad.

Look for an example of "federal prose." It need not be, of course, actually "federal"; state and municipal prose is likely to be no better, and one can find much the same sort of thing in textbooks and college catalogues. Analyze what you find and reduce a paragraph or two to "non-federal" or "anti-federal" prose.

Who Flang That Ball?

W. F. MIKSCH

My assignment was to interview Infield Ingersoll, one-time shortstop for the Wescosville Wombats and now a radio sports announcer. Dizzy Dean, Red Barber and other sportscasters had taken back seats since the colorful Ingersoll had gone on the air. The man had practically invented a new language.

"I know just what you're gonna ask," Infield began. "You wanna know how come I use all them ingrammatical expressions like 'He swang at a high one.' You think I'm illitrut."

"No, indeed," I said. Frankly, I *had* intended to ask him what effect he thought his extraordinary use of the King's English might have on future generations of radio listeners.

But a gleam in Infield's eyes when he said "illitrut" changed my mind. "What I'd really like to get," I said, "is the story of how you left baseball and became a sportscaster."

Infield looked pleased. "Well," he said, "it was the day us Wombats plew the Pink Sox . . ."

"Plew the Pink Sox?" I interrupted. "Don't you mean played?"

Infield's look changed to disappointment. "Slay, slew. Play, plew. What's the matter with that?"

NO THINKING THIS WAY "Slay is an irregular verb," I pointed out.

"So who's to say what's regular or irregular? English teachers! Can an English teacher bat three hundred?"

He paused belligerently, and then went on. "What I'm tryin' to do is easify the languish. I make all regular verbs irregular. Once they're all irregular, then it's just the same like they're all regular. That way I don't gotta stop and think."

He had something there. "Go on with your story," I said.

"Well, it was the top of the fifth, when this Sox batter wang out a high pop fly. I raught for it."

"Raught?"

"Past tense of verb to Reach. Teach, taught. Reach,—"

"Sorry," I said. "Go ahead."

"Anyhow I raught for it, only the sun blound me."

"You mean blinded?"

"Look," Infield said patiently, "you wouldn't say a pitcher winded up, would you? So there I was, blound by the sun, and the ball just nuck the tip of my glove—that's nick, nuck; same congregation as stick, stuck. But luckily I caught it just as it skam the top of my shoe."

"Skam? Could that be the past tense of to skim?"

"Yeah, yeah, same as swim, swam. You want this to be a English lesson or you wanna hear my story?"

"Your story please, Mr. Ingersoll."

"Okay. Well, just then the umpire cell, 'Safe!' Naturally I was surprose. Because I caught that fly, only the ump cell the runner safe."

"Cell is to call as fell is to fall, I suppose?" I inquired.

"Right. Now you're beginning to catch on." Infield regarded me happily as if there was now some hope for me. "So I yold at him, 'Robber! That decision smold!'"

"Yell, yold. Smell, smold," I mumbled. "Same idea as tell, told."

Infield rumbled on, "I never luck that umpire anyway."

"Hold it!" I cried. I finally had tripped this backhand grammarian. "A moment ago, you used nuck as the past for nick, justifying it by the verb to stick. Now you use luck as a verb. Am I to assume by this that luck is the past tense of to lick?"

NOBODY LUCK HIM   "Luck is past for like. To like is a regular irregular verb of which there are several such as strike, struck. Any farther questions or should I go on?"

"Excuse me," I said, "you were saying you never luck that umpire."

"And neither did the crowd. Everyone thrould at my courage. I guess I better explain thrould," Infield said thoughtfully. "Thrould comes from thrill just like would comes from will. Got that? Now to get back to my story: 'Get off the field, you bum, and no back talk!' the umpire whoze."

"Whoze?"

"He had asthma," Infield pointed out patiently.

I saw through it instantly. Wheeze, whoze. Freeze, froze.

"And with those words, that ump invote disaster. I swang at him and smeared him with a hard right that lood square on his jaw."

"Lood? Oh, I see—Stand, stood. Land, lood—it lood on his jaw."

"Sure. He just feld up and went down like a light. As he reclone on the field, he pept at me out of his good eye."

"so I quat"   "Now wait. What's this pept?" I asked.

"After you sleep, you've did what?" Infield inquired.

"Why, slept—oh, he peeped at you, did he?"

"You bet he pept at me. And in that peep I saw it was curtains for me in the league henceforward. So I beat him to it and just up and quat."

"Sit, sat. Quit—well, that gets you out of baseball," I said. "Only you still haven't told me how you got to be on radio and television."

"I guess that'll have to wait," Infield said, "on account I gotta hurry now to do a broadcast."

As he shade my hand good-by, Infield grun and wank at me.

DISCUSSION

Miksch is having fun with what might happen if an active and energetic but unlearned person applied logic to English verbs. As Infield Ingersoll says, "I make all regular verbs irregular." Miksch uses the device of an interview, as though he were a reporter, and thus recounts his meeting with Ingersoll in the first person. The device is extended and given form as Ingersoll supposedly is telling the interviewer how he came to leave baseball and become a sportscaster.

Ingersoll is really doing just the opposite of what users of the language have been doing for years. We have been tending to make our irregular verbs regular; Ingersoll is attempting to make the regular verbs irregular. Which is the better method? Try Ingersoll's system on some verbs. Which is correct, "dived" or "dove," "swum" or "swam," "awaked" or "awoke"?

Contrast the effect of language like Ingersoll's with that discussed in one of the other essays of this section; which is easier to understand? Once you see what system Ingersoll is following, how much trouble do you have in understanding him? Which method is more likely to lead to serious failure of communication, Ingersollese or Gobbledygook?

6

Advice on How to Write

The following essays contain some do's and don'ts, although perhaps not in the manner you might expect from a textbook on English. Each author is concerned that we express ourselves more effectively in our native language; a serious purpose underlies each selection. As you read, note the points made; when you have finished you will be able to answer a question like, "What does Thurber advise?" A particular question might be, "Does the author take his own advice?"

Our National Mania for Correctness

DONALD J. LLOYD

Every now and then the editors of the university presses let out a disgruntled bleat about the miserable writing done by scholars, even those who are expert in literary fields; and from time to time there are letters and editorials in our national reviews bewailing some current academic malpractice with the English language. At present, even *PMLA* (the Publications of the Modern Language Association), traditionally the repository of some of the worst writing done by researchers, is trying to herd its authors toward more lucid exposition. And at two recent meetings of the august Mediaeval Academy, one at Boston and one at Dumbarton Oaks, bitter remarks were passed about the failure of specialists in the Middle Ages to present their findings in some form palatable to the general reader, so that he can at least understand what they are writing about.

Even admitting that a really compelling style is the result of years of cultivation, much scholarly writing is certainly worse than it needs to be. But it is not alone in this. Generally speaking, the writing of literate Americans whose primary business is not writing but something else is pretty bad. It is muddy, backward, convoluted and self-strangled; it is only too obviously the product of a task approached unwillingly and accomplished without satisfaction or zeal. Except for the professionals among us, we Americans are hell on the English language. I am not in touch with the general run of British writing by non-professionals, but I suspect that it is nothing to make those islanders smug, either.

Futhermore, almost any college professor, turning the spotlight with some relief from himself and his colleagues to his students, will agree that their writing stinks to high heaven, too. It is a rare student who can write what he has to write with simplicity, lucidity and euphony, those qualities singled out by Somerset Maugham; far more graduating seniors are candidates for a remedial clinic than can pass a writing test with honors. And freshman writing is forever the nightmare of the teachers of composition, as it would be of their colleagues if the latter could not escape to the simple inanities of their objective tests.

Yet it was not always so. I have on my desk a little manuscript from the fourteenth century written by an unknown author, which I am in the process of editing. When I read it to one of my classes, as I occasionally do, with no more modernization than my own Great Lakes pronunciation and the substitution of a word for one which has become obsolete, it is a simple, clear and engaging document. "Where is any man nowadays that asketh how I shall love God and my fellow-Christians?" it begins. "How I shall flee sin and serve God truly as a true Christian man should? What man is there that will learn the true law of God, which he biddeth every Christian man to keep upon pain of damnation in hell without end? . . . Unnethe [scarcely] is there any lewd man or lewd woman that can rightly well say his Pater Noster, his Ave Maria, and his Creed, and sound the words out readily as they should. But when they play Christmas games about the fire, therein will they not fail. Those must be said out without stumbling for dread of smiting. But if a lewd man should be smited now for each failing that he maketh in saying of his Pater Noster, his Ave Maria, and his Creed, I trowe he should be smited at the full." And so on, to the beautiful poetic line, "Then think it not heavy to dwell with thy mother in her wide house, thou that laist in the strait chamber of her womb." The spelling in the original is hectic, and the capitalization and punctuation sporadic, to say the least.

Yet there was a man who knew what he had to say and set out about saying it, with no nonsense and no fumbling. He aimed for his audience and, judging by the dog-ears and sweat-marks on the book, which is about the size of one of our pocket books, he hit it. Why cannot we do as well in our time? Indeed, the eighteenth century was about the last age in which almost any man, if he was literate at all, could set down his thoughts—such as they were—so that they did not have to be excavated by the reader. We have an abundance of letters, diaries, pamphlets, and other papers from that period, and they are well written. It was the age, we may recall, not only of Boswell and Johnson, but of Pepys and Franklin as well, and of a host of other men whose main legacy to us was a simple, direct workmanlike style, sufficient to the man and to the occasion, which said what it had to say and said it well. With the end of that century we go into the foggy, foggy darkness, and God knows whether we shall ever find our way out of it—as a people, that is, as a nation of thinking men and women with something to say.

Nevertheless, there is no question what makes our writing bad, or what we shall have to do to better it. We shall simply have to isolate and root out a monomania which now possesses us, which impedes all language study and inhibits all mastery of our native tongue—all mastery, that is, on paper; for as speakers of English, we Americans are loving and effective cultivators of our expression. I recall the gas station attendant who was filling my car. The gasoline foamed to the top of the tank, and he shut off the pump. "Whew!" I said, "that nearly went over." "When you see whitecaps," he replied, "you better stop." "You better had," I said, lost in admiration. But if you had given him a pencil, he would have chewed the end off before he got one word on paper.

The demon which possesses us is our mania for correctness. It dominates our minds from the first grade to the graduate school; it is the first and often the only thing we think of when we think of our language. Our spelling must be "correct"—even if the words are ill-chosen; our "usage" must be "correct"—even though any possible substitute expression, however crude, would be perfectly clear; our punctuation must be "correct"—even though practices surge and change with the passing of years, and differ from book to book, periodical to periodical. Correct! That's what we've got to be, and the idea that we've got to be correct rests like a soggy blanket on our brains and our hands whenever we try to write.

This mania for correctness is another legacy from the eighteenth century, but it did not get a real grip on us until well into the nineteenth. Its power over us today is appalling. Among my other tasks, I teach advanced courses in the English language to students preparing to teach. Most of these are seniors and graduate students, and in the summer especially, there is a sprinkling of older men and women, experienced teachers, who are sweating out a master's degree. They have had courses in "English" throughout their schooling. But of the nature and structure of the English language, the nature of language habits, the relation of speech to writing, and the differences in usage which arise from dialect and from differing occupational and educational demands —of all these, they know nothing at all. Nor do they come to me expecting to learn about these. They want to know two things: what correct usage is and how you beat it into the kids' heads. That there are other considerations important to an English teacher is news to many of them. What they get from me is a good long look at their language.

To trace this monolithic concentration on usage is to pursue a vicious circle, with the linguists on the outside. The literate public seems to get it from the English teachers, and the teachers get it from the public. The attitudes and pronouncements on language of a Jacques Barzun, a Wilson Follett, a Bernard De Voto, or a Norman Lewis ("How Correct Must Correct English Be?") mean more to English teachers than anything said by the most distinguished professional students of language—such as Leonard Bloomfield, Robert Hall or Charles Carpenter Fries. Correct usage is pursued and discussed, furthermore, without much reference to the actual writing of literary men. Now and again I amuse myself by blue-penciling a current magazine such as the *Saturday Review* or *Collier's* against the rules. I have to report that error is rampant, if variation is to be considered error. The boys just don't seem to pay attention to the rules. Moreover, having seen some of their first drafts, I am pretty sure that what conformity they do display is the work of their wives, secretaries, editors, proofreaders and typesetters, rather than their own. It takes a determined effort to beat the old Adam out of a readable manuscript.

Thus it is only the determined, consciously creative professional who can build his work on the actual language of men. In a recent issue of the *Saturday Review,* I stumbled on a quotation from Wolfgang Langewiesche. "Well, it isn't crowned by no castle, that's for sure," he wrote, "and by no cathedral either." My eyes popped, and I read it again. I liked it. It looked right; it sounded right; it had a fine Chaucerian swing to it. But I bet it cost him some blood and a fifth of Scotch to get it into print. In my own limited publication, I find "a historical" changed to "an historical," all my "further's" changed to "farther" and all my "farther's" to "further," "than us" watered down to "than we," and many, many more. How E. M. Forster got by with "the author he thinks," and got it reprinted in a freshman handbook a few pages along from the prohibition of such locutions baffles me. A phony standardization of usage appears in print, the work of editors unconscious of the ultimate meaning of what they do.

The result of all this is that a wet hand of fear rests on the heart of every nonprofessional writer who merely has a lot of important knowledge to communicate. He writes every sentence with a self-conscious horror of doing something wrong. It is always a comfort to him if he can fit himself into some system, such as that of a business or governmental office which provides him with a model. It is thus that gobbledegook comes into being. I once braced a distinguished sociologist, a student of occupational myths and attitudes, about the convoluted, mainly nominal turgidity of his writing. He apparently admitted verbs into his sentences the way we admit DP's into the United States, reluctantly and with pain. In speech he was racy, confident and compelling, a brilliant lecturer. "It's the only way I can get my work into the periodicals," he told me blandly. "If it's clear and simple, they don't think it's scholarly." With what relief the pedagogues subside into pedagese!

If we really want to get good writing from people who know things, so that we can come to learn what they know as easily as we learn from their talk, we can do it in a generation or so. In school and out, in print and out, we can leave usage to its natural nurse, the unforced imitation of the practices which are actually current among educated people. We can use our English courses in school and college, not to give drill on questionable choices among common alternatives, demanding that one be taken as right and the others as wrong, but to give practice in reading and writing. We can learn to read and write for the idea, and go for the idea without regard for anything else. Then our young people will come to maturity confidently using their pencils to find out what they think and get it down on paper; then our scholars will come to write simply, clearly and brilliantly what they brilliantly know.

In our speech we have arrived, I think, at a decency of discourse which is conducive to effective expression. We listen, with a grave courteous attention, to massive patterns of speaking different from our own because they come from differences in dialect and social status; we listen without carping and without a mean contempt. Furthermore, we participate; we go with a speaker through halts and starts, over abysses of construction, filling in the lacunae without hesitation; we discount inadvertencies and disregard wrong words and we arrive in genial good will with the speaker at his meaning. In this atmosphere, our speech has thrived, and the ordinary American is in conversation a confident, competent expressive being. In writing he is something else again.

No one flourishes in an atmosphere of repression. It is possible, of course, for a person with special aptitudes and a special drive to bull his way past the prohibitions and achieve an individual style. But with the negative attitude that attends all our writing, those whose main interest lies elsewhere are inhibited by fear of "error" and the nagging it stirs up from setting pen to paper, until the sight of a blank white page gives them the shakes. It is no wonder that their expression is halting and ineffective. They cannot fulfill the demands of a prissy propriety and trace the form of an idea at the same time. They thus arrive at adulthood victims of the steely eye of Mr. Sherwin Cody, whose bearded face stares at them from the countless ads for his correspondence school, demanding, "Do YOU make these mistakes in English?" The locutions he lists are not mistakes, and Mr. Cody knows they are not; but his readers do not know it, and they do not know that they don't matter anyway.

For usage doesn't matter. What matters is that we get done what we have to do, and get said what we have to say. Sufficient conformity is imposed upon us by the patterns of our language and by the general practices of its users so that we do not have to run the idea of conformity into the ground by carping about trivial erratics in expression. Why in this matter of language alone complete conformity should be considered a virtue—except to typists, printers and typesetters—it is difficult to see (unless, perhaps, we are using it as a covert and pusillanimous means of establishing our own superiority). In our other concerns in life, we prize individuality; why in this one matter we should depart from a principle that otherwise serves us well is a puzzle for fools and wise men to ponder, especially since there is no general agreement on what to conform to, and one man's correctness is another's error. Not until we come to our senses—teachers, editors, writers and readers together—and stop riding each other's backs, will the casual, brisk, colorful, amused, ironic and entertaining talk of Americans find its way into print. We should all be happy to see it there.

DISCUSSION

Some readers are likely to be disturbed and even shocked by Lloyd, for if he is correct then their English teachers have often been wrong. Besides what he has to say, his very way of saying it would be severely blue-penciled by many teachers. Such expressions as "we Americans are hell on the English language," "teachers who are sweating out a master's degree," and "but I bet it cost him some blood and a fifth of Scotch" would get many students into difficulty if used in themes. Yet we learn that one of Lloyd's jobs is to teach people who are English teachers.

What is Lloyd saying? Where can you find his prescription, his advice about what to do? He gives a signal in the opening sentence of a paragraph, with "If we really want to get good writing from people who know things . . . ," which naturally leads us to expect that he will then go on to tell us what we must do if we "want to get good writing from people who know things."

What do you think of his comparison between American writing and American speech? Do you agree that "the ordinary American is in conversation a confident, competent expressive being"? What is Lloyd saying in his discussion of the vicious circle?

Notice some of the devices used by Lloyd. The sensory impressions are often vivid. What do you think of "the idea that we've got to be correct rests like a soggy blanket on our brains and our hands whenever we try to write" and "a wet hand of fear rests on the heart of every nonprofessional writer"?

Clear Only If Known

EDGAR DALE

For years I have puzzled over the inept communication of simple directions, especially those given me when touring. I ask such seemingly easy questions as: "Where do I turn off Route 40 for the by-pass around St. Louis? How do I get to the planetarium? Is this the way to the Federal Security Building?" The individual whom I hail for directions either replies "I'm a stranger here myself" or gives you in kindly fashion the directions you request. He finishes by saying pleasantly, "You can't miss it."

But about half the time you do miss it. You turn at High Street instead of Ohio Street. It was six blocks to the turn, not seven. Many persons who give directions tell you to turn right when they mean left. You carefully count the indicated five stoplights before the turn and discover that your guide meant that blinkers should be counted as stoplights. Some of the directions exactly followed turn out to be inaccurate. Your guide himself didn't know how to get there.

Now education is the problem of getting our bearings, of developing orientation, of discovering in what direction to go and how to get there. An inquiry into the problem of giving and receiving directions may help us discover something important about the educational process itself. Why do people give directions poorly and sometimes follow excellent directions inadequately?

First of all, people who give directions do not always understand the complexity of what they are communicating. They think it a simple matter to get to the Hayden Planetarium because it is simple for them. When someone says, "You can't miss it," he really means, "*I* can't miss it." He is suffering from what has been called the COIK fallacy—Clear Only If Known. It's easy to get to the place you are inquiring about if you already know how to get there.

We all suffer from the COIK fallacy. For example, during a World Series game a recording was made of a conversation between a rabid Brooklyn baseball fan and an Englishman seeing a baseball game for the first time.

The Englishman asked, "What is a pitcher?"

"He's the man down there pitching the ball to the catcher."

"But," said the Englishman, "all of the players pitch the ball and all of them catch the ball. There aren't just two persons who pitch and catch."

Later the Englishman asked, "How many strikes do you get before you are out?"

The Brooklyn fan said, "Three."

"But," replied the Englishman, "that man struck at the ball five times before he was out."

These directions about baseball, when given to the uninitiated, are clear only if known.

Try the experiment sometime of handing a person a coat and ask him to explain how to put it on. He must assume that you have lived in the tropics, have never seen a coat worn or put on, and that he is to tell you *verbally* how to do it. For example, he may say, "Pick it up by the collar." This you cannot do, since you do not know what a collar is. He may tell you to put your arm in the sleeve or to button up the coat. But you can't follow these directions because you have no previous experience with either a sleeve or a button.

The communication of teachers to pupils suffers from the COIK fallacy. An uninitiated person may think that the decimal system is easy to understand. It is—if you already know it. Some idea of the complexity of the decimal system can be gained by teachers who are asked by an instructor to understand his explanation of the duo-decimal system—a system which some mathematicians will say is even simpler than the decimal system. It is not easy to understand with just one verbal explanation, I assure you.

A teacher of my acquaintance once presented a group of parents of first-grade children with the shorthand equivalents of the first-grade reader and asked them to read this material. It was a frustrating experience. But these parents no longer thought it was such a simple matter to learn how to read in the first grade. Reading, of course, is easy if you already know how to do it.

Sometimes our directions are over-complex and introduce unnecessary elements. They do not follow the law of parsimony. Any unnecessary element mentioned when giving directions may prove to be a distraction. Think of the directions given for solving problems in arithmetic or for making a piece of furniture or for operating a camera. Have all unrelated and unnecessary items been eliminated? Every unnecessary step or statement is likely to increase the difficulty of reading and understanding the directions. There is no need to over-elaborate or labor the obvious.

In giving directions it is also easy to over-estimate the experience of our questioner. It is hard indeed for a Philadelphian to understand that anyone doesn't know where the City Hall is. Certainly if you go down Broad Street, you can't miss it. We know where it is: why doesn't our questioner?

It is easy, for example, to overestimate the historical experience of a student. The instructor often forgets that his students were toddling infants when Hoover was President. Most of them have never seen a Charlie Chaplin film. One student referred to Mary Pickford as Douglas Fairbanks' father's wife. Events that the instructor has immediately experienced have only been read or heard about by the student. What was immediate knowledge to the instructor is mediated knowledge to the student.

We are surprised to discover that many college freshmen do not know such words as *abrogate, abscond, accrue, effigy, enigma, epitome, exigency, hierarchy, lucrative, pernicious, ruminate, fallacious, salient, codify, coerce,* and *cognizance.* College professors are surprised to discover that even their abler students do not know such words as *protean, shard, ad hoc, restrictive covenant,* and *prorogue.*

Another frequent reason for failure in the communication of directions is that explanations are more technical than necessary. Thus a plumber once wrote to a research bureau pointing out that he had used hydrochloric acid to clean out sewer pipes and inquired, "Was there any possible harm?" The first reply was as follows: "The efficacy of hydrochloric acid is indisputable, but the corrosive residue is incompatible with metallic permanence." The plumber then thanked them for the information approving his procedure. The dismayed research bureau tried again, saying, "We cannot assume responsibility for the production of toxic and noxious residue with hydrochloric acid and suggest you use an alternative procedure." Once more the plumber thanked them for their approval. Finally, the bureau, worried about the New York sewers, called in a third scientist who wrote: "Don't use hydrochloric acid. It eats hell out of the pipes."

Some words are not understood and others are misunderstood. For example, a woman confided to a friend that the doctor told her that she had "very close veins." A patient was puzzled as to how she could take two pills three times a day. A little girl told her mother that the superintendent of the Sunday school said he would drop them into the furnace if they missed three Sundays in succession. He had said that he would drop them from the register.

We know the vast difference between knowing how to do something and being able to communicate that knowledge to others, of being able to verbalize it. We know how to tie a bow knot but have trouble telling others how to do it.

Another difficulty in communicating directions lies in the unwillingness of a person to say that he doesn't know. Someone drives up and asks you where Oxford Road is. You realize that Oxford Road is somewhere in the vicinity and feel a sense of guilt about not even knowing the streets in your own town. So you tend to give poor directions instead of admitting that you don't know.

Sometimes we use the wrong medium for communicating our directions. We make them entirely verbal, and the person is thus required to keep them in mind until he has followed out each of the parts of the directions. Think, for example, how hard it is to remember Hanford 6-7249 merely long enough to dial it after looking it up.

A crudely drawn map, of course, would serve the purpose. Some indication of distance would also help, although many people seem unable to give adequate estimates of distances in terms of miles. A chart or a graph can often give us an idea in a glance that is communicated verbally only with great difficulty.

But we must not put too much of the blame for inadequate directions on those who give them. Sometimes the persons who ask for help are also at fault. Communication, we must remember, is a two-way process.

Sometimes an individual doesn't understand directions but thinks he does. Only when he has lost his way does he realize that he wasn't careful enough to make sure that he really did understand. How often we let a speaker or instructor get by with such mouth-filling expressions as "emotional security," "audio-visual materials," "self-realization," without asking the questions which might clear them up for us. Even apparently simple terms like "needs" or "interests" have hidden many confusions. Our desire not to appear dumb, to be presumed "in the know," prevents us from really understanding what has been said.

We are often in too much of a hurry when we ask for directions. Like many tourists, we want to get to our destination quickly so that we can hurry back home. We don't bother to savor the trip or the scenery. So we impatiently rush off before our informant has really had time to catch his breath and make sure that we understand.

Similarly, we hurry through school subjects, getting a bird's-eye view of everything and a closeup of nothing. We aim to cover the ground when we should be uncovering it, looking for what is underneath the surface.

It is not easy to give directions for finding one's way around in a world whose values and directions are changing. Ancient landmarks have disappeared. What appears to be a lighthouse on the horizon turns out to be a mirage. But those who do have genuine expertness, those who possess tested, authoritative data, have an obligation to be clear in their explanations. Whether the issue is that of atomic energy, UNESCO, the UN, of conservation of human and natural resources, clarity in the presentation of ideas is a necessity.

We must neither overestimate nor underestimate the knowledge of the inquiring traveler. We must avoid the COIK fallacy, realize that many of our communications are clear only if already known.

DISCUSSION

Professor Dale says we can understand things told us only if we already share a considerable body of knowledge with the person addressing us. Try to imagine yourself giving directions to a complete stranger on how to get from a place you know well to a place you know equally well, along a route you are very familiar with. How much do you assume he knows? Try to give the directions to the mythical man from Mars.

Dale ends with a note of caution; which part is the more important?

Ladies' and Gentlemen's Guide to Modern English Usage

JAMES THURBER

I—WHICH The relative pronoun "which" can cause more trouble than any other word, if recklessly used. Foolhardy persons sometimes get lost in which-clauses and are a never heard of again. My distinguished contemporary, Fowler, cites several tragic cases, of which the following is one: "It was rumoured that Beaconsfield intended opening the Conference with a speech in French, his pronunciation of which language leaving everything to be desired . . ." That's as much as Mr. Fowler quotes because, at his age, he was afraid to go any farther. The young man who originally got into that sentence was never found. His fate, however, was not as terrible as that of another adventurer who became involved in a remarkable which-mire. Fowler has followed his devious course as far as he safely could on foot: "Surely what applies to games should also apply to racing, the leaders of which being the very people from whom an example might well be looked for . . ." Not even Henry James could have successfully emerged from a sentence with "which," "whom," and "being" in it. The safest way to avoid such things is to follow in the path of the American author, Ernest Hemingway. In his youth he was trapped in a which-clause one time and barely escaped with his mind. He was going along on solid ground until he got into this: "It was the one thing of which, being very much afraid—for whom has not been warned to fear such things—he . . ." Being a young and powerfully built man, Hemingway was able to fight his way back to where he had started, and begin again. This time he skirted the treacherous

Reprinted by permission; copr. © 1929, 1957 The New Yorker Magazine, Inc.

morass in this way: "He was afraid of one thing. This was the one thing. He had been warned to fear such things. Everybody has been warned to fear such things." Today Hemingway is alive and well, and many happy writers are following along the trail he blazed.

What most people don't realize is that one "which" leads to another. Trying to cross a paragraph by leaping from "which" to "which" is like Eliza crossing the ice. The danger is in missing a "which" and falling in. A case in point is this: "He went up to a pew which was in the gallery, which brought him under a colored window which he loved and always quieted his spirit." The writer, worn out, missed the last "which"—the one that should come just before "always" in that sentence. But supposing he had got it in! We would have: "He went up to a pew which was in the gallery, which brought him under a colored window which he loved and which always quieted his spirit." Your inveterate whicher in this way gives the effect of tweeting like a bird or walking with a crutch, and is not welcome in the best company.

It is well to remember that one "which" leads to two and that two "whiches" multiply like rabbits. You should never start out with the idea that you can get by with one "which." Suddenly they are all around you. Take a sentence like this: "It imposes a problem which we either solve, or perish." On a hot night, or after a hard day's work, a man often lets himself get by with a monstrosity like that, but suppose he dictates that sentence bright and early in the morning. It comes to him typed out by his stenographer and he instantly senses that something is the matter with it. He tries to reconstruct the sentence, still clinging to the "which," and gets something like this: "It imposes a problem which we either solve, or which, failing to solve, we must perish on account of." He goes to the water-cooler, gets a drink, sharpens his pencil, and grimly tries again. "It imposes a problem which we either solve or which we don't solve and . . . " He begins once more: "It imposes a problem which we either solve, or which we do not solve, and from which . . ." The more times he does it the more "whiches" he gets. The way out is simple: "We must either solve this problem, or perish." Never monkey with "which." Nothing except getting tangled up in a typewriter ribbon is worse.

II—THE PERFECT INFINITIVE It is easy enough to say that a
person should live in such a way as to avoid the perfect infinitive
after the past conditional, but it is another matter to do it. The
observance of the commonest amenities of life constantly leads us
into that usage. Let us take a typical case. A gentleman and his
wife, calling on friends, find them not at home. The gentleman
decides to leave a note of regret couched in a few well-chosen
words, and the first thing he knows he is involved in this: "We
would have liked to have found you in." Reading it over, the gentleman is assailed by the suspicion that he has too many "haves,"
and that the whole business has somehow been put too far into the
past. His first reaction is to remedy this by dating the note: "9 p.m.
Wednesday, Jan. 21, 1931." This at once seems too formal, and
with a sigh he starts in again on the sentence itself. That is where
he makes a fatal mistake. The simplest way out, as always, is to
seek some other method of expressing the thought. In this case the
gentleman should simply dash off, "Called. You were out. Sorry,"
and go home to bed. What he does, however, is to lapse into a pro-
found study of this particular grammatical situation, than which
there is no more hazardous mental occupation. His wife should,
above all things, not choose this time to nag at him, or hurry him.
His condition now calls for the utmost kindness and consideration.

First the victim will change the sentence to: "We would have
liked to find you in." Now as a matter of fact, this is correct (bar-
ring the use of "would" instead of "should"), but, alas, the gentleman does not realize it. Few people ever do realize it. This is
because the present infinitive, "to find," seems to imply success.
They therefore fall back on the perfect infinitive, "to have found,"
because it implies that the thing hoped for did not come to pass.
They have fallen back on it so often that, after the ordinary past
tenses, its use has come to be counted as idiomatic, even though it
is incorrect. After past conditionals, however—such as our gentleman caller has got into—the use of the perfect infinitive is not even
idiomatic. It is just dangerous.

The gentleman, with two variants on his hands, takes to mum-
bling them to himself, first one and then the other—"We would
have liked to have found you in," "We would have liked to find

you in." After he does this several times, both expressions begin to sound meaningless. They don't make any sense at all, let alone make precise sense. His mental feeling is analogous to the terror that strikes into children's minds when they get to repeating some common word, like "saucer," over and over again, until it sounds idiotic and legendary. At this point it would be infinitely better not to leave any note at all, but the gentleman's education and his strength of mind have been challenged. He takes an envelope out of his pocket and grimly makes a list of all the possible combinations, thus getting: "We would have liked to have found," "We would have like to find," "We would like to have found," and "We would like to find." A dull pain takes him back of the ears. This is the danger sign, and his wife should have the presence of mind to summon assistance, for he is now out of hand and uncontrollable. What she does, however, is to say, "Here, let me write it." He instantly snarls, "I'm no child" or "Get away" or some such thing, and his difficulties are added to by the quarrel which follows. At length he has the bright inspiration of going into the hope clauses and turns out: "We had hoped to have been able to have found." If he has married the right kind of woman, she will hastily scratch a brief word on a calling card, shove it under the door, and drag her husband away. Otherwise he will sink rapidly into a serious mental state, from which it may take him weeks to emerge.

There is a simple rule about past conditionals which will prevent a lapse into that deep contemplation which is so often fatal. After "would have liked," "would have hoped," "would have feared," etc., use the present infinitive. The implication of nonfulfillment is inherent in the governing verb itself, that is, in the "would have liked," etc. You don't have to shade the infinitive to get a nice note of frustration. Let it alone. Dr. Fowler himself says: "Sometimes a writer, dimly aware that 'would have liked to have done' is wrong, is yet so fascinated by the perfect infinitive that he clings to that at all cost." That's what it is—a fascination—like a cobra's for a bird. Avoid the perfect infinitive after the past conditional as you would a cobra.

III—THE SUBJUNCTIVE MOOD   The importance of correct grammar in the home can not be overestimated. Two young people should make sure that each is rhetorically sound before they get married, because grammatical precision, particularly in mood, is just as important as anything else. Rhetoric and sex, in fact, are so closely related that when one becomes confused they both become confused. Take the subjunctive. Fowler, in his book on modern English usage, says the subjunctive is dying, but adds that there are still a few truly living uses, which he groups under "Alives, Revivals, Survivals, and Arrivals." Curiously enough, he leaves out Departures, which it seems to me are just as important as Arrivals. Let us examines the all too common domestic situation where the husband arrives just after another gentleman has departed—or just after he thinks another gentleman has departed (Suppositional Departures lead to just as much bitterness, and even more subjunctives, than Actual Departures).

The wife, in either case, is almost sure to go into the subjunctive —very likely before any accusation is made. Among the most common subjunctives which she will be inclined to use are those of indignation and hauteur, such as "Be that as it may," "Far be it from me," etc. For the moment, she is safe enough in the subjunctive, because her husband has probably gone into it, too, using "Would God I were," "If there be justice," and so on. Wives select the subjunctive usually because it is the best mood in which to spar for time, husbands because it lends itself most easily to ranting and posturing. As long as they both stay in it they are safe. Misunderstandings are almost certain to arise, however, when the husband goes into the indicative, as he is pretty sure to do. He usually does this preparatory to dismissing his suspicions, a step toward which every husband is impelled by his natural egotism. First he will begin with a plain past-tense indicative if-clause— just to show that he knows who the man is—prior to dismissing him.

"If George Spangrell was here," the husband will begin, lighting a cigarette, "I . . ."

"Well, what would you do if he *were?*" demands the wife.

The confusion, which begins at this point, is pretty intricate. The husband has gone into the indicative, but his wife has stayed in the subjunctive and, furthermore, she thinks that he is still there, too. Thus she thinks he intended to say: "If George Spangrell was here [that is, now] I would tell him what I think of him, the low scoundrel." There is no excuse for a wife prematurely imputing such a suspicion or such a rhetorical monstrosity to her husband. What he probably intended to say was merely something like this: "If George Spangrell was here, I wouldn't like it, but of course I know he wasn't, dear." However, misunderstandings now begin to pile up. The husband is instantly made suspicious by her "What would you do if he *were?*" He considers her "were" tantamount to "is." (This quick-tempered construction, of course, makes the "would" in his wife's sentence ridiculous, for, had she meant "is" instead of "were," she would have substituted "will" for "would.") The situation is much too involved now, however, for the husband to make an effort to parse anything. He instantly abandons all grammatical analysis, and begins to look about, peering into the wardrobe, swishing under beds with a cane or umbrella.

His wife now has the advantage of him, not only in mood, but in posture. A woman must naturally view with disdain and contempt any man who is down on all fours unless he has taken that position for the purpose of playing horse with some children—an extenuation which we need not discuss here. To meet her on even terms, the husband should walk, not crawl, from wardrobe to chaise-longue, using the mandatory subjunctive in a firm voice, as follows: "If anyone be in (or under) there, let him come out!" ["Come out" is better here than "emerge" because stronger, but a husband should not fall into the colloquial "Come on out of that!" He may, however, if he so wishes, address the gentleman, whether he be present or not, as "Spangrell" but never "Mr. Spangrell" (Hypocritical Dignification) and certainly never as "George"— the use of the given name being in extreme bad taste where no endearment is intended.]

The wife of course will resent all these goings-on, and the quarrel that results will probably last late into the night.

There are several ways to prevent a situation like this. In the first place, when a husband says "was" a wife should instantly respond with "wasn't." Most husbands will take a "wasn't" at its face value, because it preserves their egotism and self-respect. On the other hand, "if . . . were" is always dangerous. Husbands have come to know that a wife's "if . . . were" usually means that what she is presenting as purely hypothetical is, in reality, a matter of fact. Thus, if a wife begins, one evening after an excellent dinner, "Dear, what would you do, if I were the sort of woman who had, etc.," her husband knows full well that it is going to turn out that she is the sort of woman who has. Husbands are suspicious of all subjunctives. Wives should avoid them. Once a woman has "if . . . were'd" a Mr. Spangrell, her husband is, nine times out of ten, going to swish under the chaise-longue. Even if he finds no one, the situation becomes extremely awkward, and there is of course always the plaguey hundredth chance that he may discover a strange cane or pair of gloves.

The best of all ways out is for the husband to go instantly into the future indicative and say, with great dignity, "I shall go down to the drugstore." Ordinarily, his wife would reply, "Oh, no you won't," but with all the doubt and suspicion in the air, she will be inclined to humor him and let him have his way. She is certain to, if Spangrell is in the clothes hamper.

DISCUSSION

Thurber is having fun with language, a pleasant activity when one knows as much about the subject as did James Thurber. But even if one lacks such knowledge, it should be easy to see that the matter of using a language can be enjoyable. Perhaps you can think of ways to express something in a way that, while not false, will lead the reader away from the scent, will lead him to look at the subject as you want him to do. Concoct an explanation of why you arrived home so late, why the fender of the car is crumpled, why the window is cracked, why the theme is not ready at the assigned time. But do so in a Thurber-way.

7

Writers on Writing

THE FOLLOWING SELECTIONS present four modern writers, three American and one Irish, on the subject of writing in general and their own work in particular. The two Nobel Prize winners, Ernest Hemingway and William Faulkner, died just a few years ago; the other two are still at work. The selection on Faulkner is a transcription of a taped interview conducted while Mr. Faulkner was at the University of Virginia. Harvey Breit presents a kind of self-interview with Hemingway, written shortly after the appearance of *The Old Man and the Sea,* the last novel to be published in Hemingway's lifetime. The interviews with Truman Capote and Frank O'Connor are part of the famous series made by the *Paris Review.* They are all, then, quite informal and spontaneous; they are not essays. Each reflects the personality of its subject; each is useful in approaching the work of its subject.

Faulkner in the University

Edited by
FREDERICK L. GWYNN
and JOSEPH L. BLOTNER

SESSION EIGHT, MARCH 13, 1958

Q. Mr. Faulkner, this is sort of a question of motivation for the writer. Many of the best Southern writers write about the degeneration of the old aristocracy and the determination to live and to think according to the old traditions and standards. Now do you think that this continued determination on the part of those around him causes the writer to revolt against this system, and accordingly is it a—does this attitude—does it furnish a motivation for writing?

A. It does, in that that is a condition of environment. It's something that is handed to the writer. He is writing about people in the terms that he's most familiar with. That is, it could have sociological implications, but he's not too interested in that. He's writing about people. He is using the material which he knows, the tools which are at hand, and so he uses the instinct or the desire of whatever you will call it of the old people to be reactionary and tory, to stick to the old ways. It's simply a condition, and since it is a condition it lives and breathes, and it is valid as material.

Q. Sir, I believe you were in Europe in 1923 at the same time Anderson and Hemingway and others [were]. At that time, did you associate with them, and if not, was there any specific reason why you were not thrown together, and do you think the group was influenced or influenced each other in any way from their association?

A. They may have. I think the artist is influenced by all in his environment. He's maybe more sensitive to it because he has got to get the materials, the lumber that he's going to build his edifice. I—at that time I didn't think of myself as a writer, I was a tramp then, and I didn't—I wasn't interested in literature nor literary people. They were—I was—there at the same time, I knew Joyce, I knew of Joyce, and I would go to some effort to go to the café that he inhabited to look at him. But that was the only literary man that I remember seeing in Europe in those days. . . .

Q. Sir, it has been argued that "A Rose for Emily" is a criticism of the North, and others have argued saying that it is a criticism of the South. Now, could this story, shall we say, be more properly classified as a criticism of the times?

A. Now that I don't know, because I was simply trying to write about people. The writer uses environment—what he knows— and if there's a symbolism in which the lover represented the North and the woman who murdered him represents the South, I don't say that's not valid and not there, but it was no intention of the writer to say, "Now let's see, I'm going to write a piece in which I will use a symbolism for the North and another symbol for the South," that he was simply writing about people, a story which he thought was tragic and true because it came out of the human heart, the human aspiration, the human—the conflict of conscience with glands, with the Old Adam. It was a conflict not between the North and the South so much as between, well you might say, God and Satan.

Q. Sir, just a little more on that thing. You say it's a conflict be-tween God and Satan. Well, I don't quite understand what you mean. Who is—did one represent, the—

A. The conflict was in Miss Emily, that she knew that you do not murder people. She had been trained that you do not take a lover. You marry, you don't take a lover. She had broken all the laws of her tradition, her background, and she had finally broken the law of God too, which says you do not take human life. And she knew she was doing wrong, and that's why her own life was wrecked. Instead of murdering one lover, and then to go on and take another and when she used him up to murder him, she was expiating her crime.

Q. . . . She did do all the things that she had been taught not to do, and being a sensitive sort of a woman, it was sure to have told on her, but do you think it's fair to feel pity for her, because in a way she made her adjustment, and it seems to have wound up in a happy sort of a way—certainly tragic, but maybe it suited her just fine.

A. Yes, it may have, but then I don't think that one should with-hold pity simply because the subject of the pity, object of pity, is pleased and satisfied. I think the pity is in the human striving against its own nature, against its own conscience. That's what deserves the pity. It's not the state of the individual, it's man in conflict with his heart, or with his fellows, or with his environ-ment—that's what deserves the pity. It's not that the man suffered, or that he fell off the house, or was run over by the train. It's that he was—that man is trying to do the best he can with his desires and impulses against his own moral conscience, and the conscience of, the social conscience of, his time and his place—the little town he must live in, the family he's a part of. . . .

Q. In *The Bear*, Mr. Faulkner, was there a dog, a real lion?

A. Yes, there was. I can remember that dog—I was about the age of that little boy—and he belonged to our pack of bear and deer dogs, and he was a complete individualist. He didn't love anybody. The other dogs were all afraid of him, he was a savage, but he did love to run the bear. Yes, I remember him quite well. He was mostly airedale, he had some hound and Lord only knows what else might have been in him. He was a tremendous big brute—stood about that high, must have weighed seventy-five or eighty pounds.

Q. In any bear hunt that Lion participated in, did he ever perform a heroic action like the one in the story?

A. No, not really. There's a case of the sorry, shabby world that don't quite please you, so you create one of your own, so you make Lion a little braver than he was, and you make the bear a little more of a bear than he actually was. I am sure that Lion could have done that and would have done it, and it may be at times when I wasn't there to record the action, he did do things like that.

Q. This question is also concerned with *The Bear*. In conclusion of the story, Ike McCaslin finds Boon destroying his rifle. Now I was wondering if this incident just showed that Boon could not, shall we say, compete with the mechanical age, or whether this was showing the end of an order, the fact that Lion and old Ben were dead, that the hunters weren't returning to the cabin any more, and the land had been sold to a lumber company.

A. A little of both. It was that Boon, with the mentality of a child, a boy of sixteen or seventeen, couldn't cope not only with the mechanical age but he couldn't cope with any time. Also, to me it underlined the heroic tragedy of the bear and the dog by the last survivor being reduced to the sort of petty comedy of someone trying to patch up a gun in order to shoot a squirrel. That made the tragedy of the dog and the bear a little more poignant to me. That's the sort of *tour de force* that I think the writer's entitled to use. . . .

Q. I know that you stated that you don't read the critics regarding your own work. However, I wonder what ideas you have regarding the aims or the proper function of a literary critic, not only of your works, but shall we say of others as well.

A. I would say he has a valid function, a very important function, but to me he's a good deal like the minister— you don't need to listen to him unless you need him, and I in my own case, I know, I have already decided about the value of my work. There's nothing anybody can tell me I don't know about it, and the critic, nor I either, can improve it any by that time and the only way to improve it is to write one that will be better next time, and so I'm at that and I probably just don't have time to read the critics. . . .

Q. What would you have done if they had asked you to make changes [in your first novel]?

A. Well, I don't know, because I had lost my bootlegging job of the—I believe the Federal people finally caught him, and I had a job as an ordinary seaman in a freighter then. I spent the next year or two on ships, and by that time I was working on another book, and so I got out of touch with this one. I don't—I reckon I would have changed it probably if the publisher had said, "If you make a few changes, we'll print it." I probably would.

Q. Sir, I think you said that you haven't yet achieved your own personal goal as a writer. What is that goal and is it likely that you will succeed in achieving it?

A. That's difficult to say. It's when I have done something that, to use Hemingway's phrase, makes me feel good, that is completely satisfactory, maybe that will be the goal, and I hope just a little I'll never quite do that because if I do there won't be any reason to go on writing, and I'm too old to take up another hobby. It's—I think that a writer wants to make something that he knows that a hundred or two hundred or five hundred, a thousand years later will make people feel what they feel when they read Homer, or read Dickens or Balzac, Tolstoy, that that's probably his goal. I don't think that he bothers until he gets old like this and has a right to spend a lot of time talking about it to put that into actual words. But probably that's what he wants, that really the writer doesn't want success, that he knows he has a short span of life, that the day will come when he must pass through the wall of oblivion, and he wants to leave a scratch on that wall—Kilroy was here—that somebody a hundred, a thousand years later will see.

Q. Sir, why do you regard *The Sound and the Fury* as your best work?

A. It was the best failure. It was the one that I anguished the most over, that I worked the hardest at, that even when I knew I couldn't bring it off, I still worked at it. It's like the parent feels toward the unfortunate child, maybe. The others that have been easier to write than that, and in ways are better books than that, but I don't have the feeling toward any of them that I do toward that one, because that was the most gallant, the most magnificent failure.

Q. Mr. Faulkner, you said that even though you did not bring it off, you worked hardest at it. How do you feel that you failed to bring *The Sound and the Fury* off?

A. It don't make me feel good enough, to use Hemingway's phrase. That's a condition that probably I can't put into words, but if I ever do strike it, I will know it. I think that that's true of any writer.

Q. Well, aren't there parts of it that make you feel good enough?

A. Well, that's not enough—parts of it are not enough, it must be all, you see. You can't compromise, you know, it's either good or it ain't, there's no degrees of goodness. It's either all right or it's not all right. . . .

Q. Can you make any comment on the part that the Old General plays in *A Fable,* who seemed to me to take two distinct, different parts if not more, in the theme of Passion Week, including the Three Temptations? Would you care to elaborate at all on that character?

A. Well, to me he was the dark, splendid, fallen angel. The good shining cherubims to me are not very interesting, it's the dark, gallant, fallen one that is moving to me. He was an implement, really. What I was writing about was the trilogy of man's conscience represented by the young British Pilot Officer, the Runner, and the Quartermaster General. The one that said, "This is dreadful, terrible, and I won't face it even at the cost of my life"—that was the British aviator. The Old General who said, "This is terrible but we can bear it." The third one, the battalion Runner who said, "This is dreadful, I won't stand it, I'll do something about it." The Old General was Satan, who had been cast out of heaven, and—because God Himself feared him.

Q. Well, what—the thing that has puzzled me was that, going back, as far as I could gather, he also had been the father of the Corporal.

A. Yes, that's right.

Q. And that is what has somewhat puzzled me in the allegorical—

A. That was a part of Satan's fearsomeness, that he could usurp the legend of God. That was what made him so fearsome and so powerful, that he could usurp the legend of God and then discard God. That's why God feared him.

Q. Mr. Faulkner, would you care to say anthing about the allegorical function of the horse in *A Fable?* He seems to have some very complex and interesting characteristics.

A. Not to me, no. That was simply another struggle between man and his conscience and his environment. The horse was simply a tool—that is, that foul and filthy Cockney ostler was still capable of love for something. That maybe if he'd had a better childhood, a better background, he might have been capable of better love, of something more worthy than a horse. But he was capable of love for one thing, that he could sacrifice to and could defend, even though it was only a horse.

Q. In the story "Red Leaves," in the Indian burial ritual, would

it have brought disgrace to that . . . whole ritual had the man-
servant committed suicide during the chase, before they caught
him?

A. No, they could still have brought his body back and immolated that. No, they were simply cleaning house, that was what
the rule said.—When the chief went back to the earth, his body
servant and his dogs and his horse went with him. No, it would
have been no disgrace. In fact, if he had done that quicker, they
would have been pleased because it would have saved them all
the trouble of tracking him back and forth through that swamp,
which they didn't want to do. They were a lazy indolent people,
and there wasn't any use of anyone causing all that trouble when
he couldn't get away.

Q. What is your purpose in writing into the first section of *The
Sound and the Fury* passages that seem disjointed in themselves if
the idea is not connected with one another?

A. That was part of the failure. It seemed to me that the book
approached nearer the dream if the groundwork of it was laid by
the idiot, who was incapable of relevancy. That's—I agree with
you too, that's a bad method, but to me it seemed the best way to
do it, that I shifted those sections back and forth to see where they
went best, but my final decision was that though that was not
right, that was the best way to do it, that was simply the groundwork of that story, as that idiot child saw it. He himself didn't
know what he was seeing. That the only thing that held him into
any sort of reality, into the world at all, was the trust that he had
for his sister, that he knew that she loved him and would defend
him, and so she was the whole world to him, and these things were
flashes that were reflected on her as in a mirror. He didn't know
what they meant.

Q. You spoke a minute ago of the writer seeking to leave some
degree of his mark on posterity. I was wondering if you think that
the effect on the artist is better today when he can somehow
achieve his immortality during his lifetime because of the communications being so much wider and greater than formerly when
perhaps the writer's fame came to him long after his death and
maybe he was the only one during his lifetime that was satisfied
with his work?

A. I don't think so. I believe the writer takes a longer view than that. He ain't too interested in what the contemporary world thinks about him. He has a longer view, that he is aimed not at Jones of 1957 but at Jones of 2057 or 4057.

Q. Well, do you think that you would have been just as satisfied if your work say had never been discovered until 4057?

A. I think so, sure, yes. Of course when they began to bring in a little money, that was nice. I liked the money, but the glory, the rest of it's not very valuable.

Q. Well, then thinking that this period doesn't matter too much, do you go back over the things, and do you still have a lot of time left to work over the ones that you've already written? Do you go back and worry about them and wish you had done them differently?

A. I wish I had done them better, but I don't have time to worry about it too much. That's just a constant thought or belief that I would like to be able to do them over again—that is, not to go back and take one single book and write another version of it, but if I could go back and take one single book and write another version of it, but if I could go back to say 1920 when I started, that I could do a better job. Of course I wouldn't, but that's an idle thought that occurs only when I haven't got anything better to do. The best thing is to write another book and do it, because it takes only one book to do it. It's not the sum of a lot of scribbling, it's one perfect book, you see. It's one single urn or shape that you want to do. . . .

Q. When you do write about people that way—well, of course, you don't have to put up with the critics, but I've noticed particularly when a new book comes out, all the Freudian implications are pulled out and all sorts of undercurrents rather than just the simple Here's what happened and—of course, there's always more to it than that, but all kinds of weird things are just pulled out of the hat and thrown around. Would that bother you, does it disturb you to have everything sort of misconstrued?

A. I can't say because I'm not aware of it. I don't read the critics. I don't know any literary people. The people I know are other farmers and horse people and hunters, and we talk about horses and dogs and guns and what to do about this hay crop or this cotton crop, not about literature. I think—I'm convinced, though, that that sort of criticism whether it's nonsensical or not is valid because it is a symptom of change, or motion, which is life, and also it's a proof that literature—art—is a living quantity in our social condition. If it were not, then there'd be no reason for people to delve and find all sorts of symbolisms and psychological strains and currents in it. And I'm quite sure that there are some writers to whom that criticism is good, that it could help them find themselves. I don't know that the critic could teach the writer anything because I'm inclined to think that nobody really can teach anybody anything, that you offer it and it's there and if it is your will or urge to learn it you do, and the writer that does need the criticism can get quite a lot of benefit from it. . . .

Q. Sir, what are the Spotted Horses symbolic of, if anything?

A. As spotted horses, I don't know. That may be symbolical, but as horses, that was—they symbolized the hope, the aspiration of the masculine part of society that is capable of doing, of committing puerile folly for some gewgaw that has drawn him, as juxtaposed to the cold practicality of the women whose spokesman Mrs. Littlejohn was when she said "Them men!" or "What fools men are!" That the man even in a society where there's a constant pressure to conform can still be taken off by the chance to buy a horse for three dollars. Which to me is a good sign, I think. I hope that man can always be tolled off that way, to buy a horse for three dollars.

Q. Mr. Faulkner, what sort of reading do you best enjoy? Do you have much time for the work of your contemporary novelists?

A. No, I don't. I haven't read a contemporary book in twenty-odd years, unless someone says, "This is a good book, I think you would like it," and so I will get that book and read it, but I've got out of the habit of keeping up with contemporaries because I never was a literary man in the sense of needing to keep abreast of the establishment of literature. To me, reading is like writing—I do it for fun. I'm not too interested in what anybody else has done, that I read books because it's fun. . . .

Q. Sir, could you suggest any books that one read first, in order to get a clearer and more comprehensive picture of your complete works, and if there are any, why these specific choices?

A. There are none. I think the best way to read—no, I can't say the best way, this is the way I read—I take the book and I can tell within two or three pages if I want to read that book now. If I don't, I put that down and I take another. I would say to take Faulkner that same way, and read a page or two until you find one that you want to read another page. It would be difficult for anyone except an expert to plot out a schedule for you. I would do it that way, I think.

Q. Sir, do you have any solution for a man to find peace if he cannot write, as you?

A. Well, I don't think the writer finds peace. If he did, he would quit writing. Maybe man is incapable of peace. Maybe that is what differentiates man from a vegetable. Though maybe the vegetable don't even find peace. Maybe there's no such thing as peace, that it is a negative quality.

Q. I am speaking of peace in his own heart.

A. Yes, well, I'm inclined to think that the only peace man knows is—he says, "Why good gracious, yesterday I was happy." That at the moment he's too busy. That maybe peace is only a condition in retrospect when the subconscious has got rid of the gnats and the tacks and the broken glass in experience and has left only the peaceful pleasant things—that was peace. Maybe peace is not is, but was.

Q. Do you enjoy reading Shakespeare? I heard you speak of Homer. I was just wondering how you felt—

A. Yes'm, I still read Shakespeare. I have a one-volume Shakespeare that I have just about worn out carrying around with me.

Q. Mr. Faulkner, I think you told somebody once that if you had a—were writing something, and had something to get up to every morning and got to work on, you'd never have to be afraid of anything in the world any more. And I wonder what you meant by that.

A. I mean by that, that fear, like so many evil things, comes mainly out of idleness, that if you have something to get up to tomorrow morning, you're too busy to pay much attention to fear. Of course, you have the fears, but you have—you don't have time to take them too seriously if you have something to get up to do tomorrow. It don't matter too much what it is, and if it's something

that you yourself believe is valid, in the sense that the artist be-
lieves what he's doing is valid in that it may do something to uplift
man's heart, not to make man any more successful, but to temporarily make him feel better than he felt before, to uplift his heart
for a moment.

Q. In *The Bear,* Mr. Faulkner, is the possession and destruction
of the wilderness a symbolic indication of any sort of corruption in
the South, and if this is true, what sort of prognostication does this
have for the future and for the South or the country as a whole?

A. Well, of course the destruction of the wilderness is not a
phenonmenon of the South, you know. That is a change that's
going on everywhere, and I think that man progresses mechani-
cally and technically much faster than he does spiritually, that
there may be something he could substitute for the ruined wilderness, but he hasn't found that. He spends more time ruining the
wilderness than he does finding something to replace it, just like
he spends more time producing more people than something good
to do with the people or to make better people out of them. That
that's to me a sad and tragic thing for the old days, the old times,
to go, providing you have the sort of background which a country
boy like me had when that was a part of my life. That I don't
want it to change, but then that's true of everyone as he grows
old. He thinks that the old times were the best times, and he
don't want it to change.

Q. Is the short story "Death Drag" based on an actual event
or experience in your life?

A. Not too much. They were—I did a little what they call barn-
storming in the early days after the War, when aeroplanes were
not too usual and people would pay a hundred dollars to be taken
for a short ride in one, but I don't remember anything that was
specifically like this. This was again a human being in conflict
with his environment and his time. This man who hated flying, but
that was what he had to do, simply because he wanted to make a
little money.

Q. What symbolic meaning did you give to the dates of *The
Sound and the Fury?*

A. Now there's a matter of hunting around in the carpenter's
shop to find a tool that will make a better chicken-house. And

probably—I'm sure it was quite instinctive that I picked out Easter, that I wasn't writing any symbolism of the Passion Week at all. I just—that was a tool that was good for the particular corner I was going to turn in my chicken-house and so I used it.

Q. Sir, you mentioned some of the Russian authors before. What do you think of Dostoevsky? Do you consider him one of the best?

A. He is one who has not only influenced me a lot, but that I have got a great deal of pleasure out of reading, and I still read him again every year or so. As a craftsman, as well as his insight into people, his capacity for compassion, he was one of the ones that any writer wants to match if he can, that he was one who wrote a good Kilroy Was Here.

Q. There's a line in "Was" that—I wonder if you would explain something about it. That Tomey's Turl says to Cass, "Any time you wants to get something done, from hoeing out a crop to getting married, just get the women folks to working at it. That all you needs to do—then all you needs to do is set down and wait." Well, that's good advice, but does he use it in this story. Does Tomey's Turl get the women-folks to work for him?

A. Well, I'm sure he would if he'd had time, but people were running him with dogs so much and harrying and harassing from pillar to post he didn't have time, but if he could have got the men to stop long enough, then Miss Sophonsiba would have settled that whole thing. She would have taken Uncle Buck home, then Tomey's Turl and Tennie could have gotten married and things would have been settled. It was the men that kept things stirred up, probably Tomey's Turl knew that soon as the dust settled, no matter what was the outcome of that poker game, Miss Sophonsiba and Uncle Buck would get married and that then he and Tennie would be let alone. . . .

Q. Mr. Faulkner, I wonder if you could comment on who you think in say two hundred years from now will be the biggest Kilroys Were Here of this century, which writers will leave the biggest Kilroy, if any?

A. I don't want to answer that question because I'm too unfamiliar with contemporary writers. I haven't read any contemporaries since the three or four of my time, and so often a remark like that in simple talk, it gets out, and someone's feelings have been hurt that the man that spoke it had no intention of hurting because he didn't even know he existed, and so for that reason I wouldn't answer that question at all. I would say that I think that Sherwood Anderson has not received the recognition that he deserves and some day will have.

Q. What about Hemingway?

A. Hemingway, now he's alive, and that's where I'd better stay out of trouble by saying nothing, you see.

Q. Would you say anything about your own writings . . . or would you hurt your own feelings?

A. No, I still haven't done it, but I intend to live to be about a hundred years old, so I've got forty more years yet. By that time I'll answer your question if you're still around.

DISCUSSION

William Faulkner was famous for his reworking of the language; he often coined words and used words in unusual ways. This, coupled with the fact that the interview here presented is a literal transcription, results in what would be termed incorrect English if offered on a college theme. Also, Faulkner was very independent: he did not hesitate to use "ain't" or "he don't."

All the stories mentioned are readily available in a variety of editions. Much Faulkner has been filmed; Faulkner did much of the film adaptation himself.

In the interview Faulkner is trying to answer the common question, "What is the story about?" Note his denial of any attempt to write sociological or psychological works. He says he is interested in people, and whatever is sociological or psychological or anything else arises from what the people do. Note his answer to the question concerning the dates of *The Sound and the Fury;* he is here using a figure of speech in an attempt to explain how the dates were chosen. Why does he do this? What is that chicken-house doing there?

What advice does William Faulkner give on how to read? Have you ever read any Faulkner; does the advice work? What about his closing remarks in view of the fact that it turned out he did not have forty more years to write, but only three?

Ernest Hemingway

HARVEY BREIT

This week Mr. Ernest Hemingway is the news truly. Not only the literary news. Like Earl Sande booting home a Derby winner, or Johnny Vander Meer pitching two no-hitters in succession, or the Manassa Mauler battering big Jess Willard, a book by Papa is front page news. This fact creates certain misunderstandings. Mr. Hemingway seems to be in the news more than he actually is only because each time he makes his move it starts talk. This is not his fault, and the people who think of Mr. Hemingway as a chap who likes moving into the spotlight are not less than dead wrong. As a matter of record, it would be difficult to find a writer who lives more privately, minding his own business and cultivating his own garden (in the best Voltairean sense of the phrase).

Well here we are too, just as meddlesome as the rest. Mr. Hemingway writes a small, fine novel, *The Old Man and the Sea*, and instead of letting him be, and being happy about it, we're after him—and there is no discharge from the war. True, we went after him equivocally, ridden by a guilt sufficient to prevent us from asking questions. We merely asked him for a statement, or a number of statements, on whatever was occupying him at the time. Pro and gallant that he is, Mr. Hemingway kicked through with a set of answers to a set of questions that he himself devised. Without further ado, then, here is Mr. Hemingway answering Mr. Hemingway:

Q. How do you feel, Mr. H.?

A. Very well, thank you.

Q. What are your plans?

A. To take a vacation, if I have any money left after taxes, and then go back to work.

Q. Where would you like to take your vacation?

A. Either out West or in Europe.

Q. Do you enjoy writing, Mr. H.?

A. Very much. But if you do it as well as you can each day, it is tiring.

Q. Do you mind talking about it?

A. I do not believe in talking about it and I try to avoid talking about it. If I have to talk about a book that I have written it destroys the pleasure I have from writing it. If the writing is any good everything there is to say has been conveyed to the reader.

Q. What about fishing?

A. I have enjoyed it ever since I can remember. But I do not enjoy talking about it except to professional fishermen. One of the reasons I quit fishing at Bimini was to avoid the nightly post mortems of the anglers. Another was because the big fish caught were wasted. No fish caught in Cuba is wasted.

Q. Do you spend much time on the sea?

A. In twenty years of my life probably half of it has been spent on the sea.

Q. Can you work while at sea?

A. Perhaps better than anywhere else. My boat, The Pilar, has no radio, no telephone and, since the war, no radio communications of any kind. You can anchor in the lee of some bay in the Gulf Stream and write on a writing board with no intrusions and you have no excuses if you fail to work well.

Q. Does your wife like the sea?

A. She loves it very much. She has never been seasick and she loves to swim and fish, all kinds of fishing, and to watch the stars at night.

Q. Do you have a happy life, Mr. Hemingway?

A. I have never heard a happy life defined. I have always been happy when I am working. If I cannot work I usually do something bad and have remorse and then my conscience makes me work. A conscience tells truths that are as uncomfortable as those a compass sometimes shows. Personally I am happy when I work hard and love someone. Since I have done both these things now for a long time I would say I have a happy life. Times have always been bad. But Walter Raleigh wrote very well the night before he climbed the steps to the scaffold erected in the Old Palace yard of Westminster. I see no reason now not to write well because the times are bad both for those who write and those who read.

DISCUSSION

It appears here that Hemingway is asking himself the kinds of questions he would expect to be asked if someone were interviewing him. Note that like Faulkner he declines to engage in much literary talk. Faulkner does discuss some meanings, whereas Hemingway says, "If the writing is any good everything there is to say has been conveyed to the reader." Compare the two endings; in one Hemingway talks of happiness, Faulkner of fear; how far apart are they?

Truman Capote

THE PARIS REVIEW

INTERVIEWER: What did you first write?

CAPOTE: Short stories. And my more unswerving ambitions still revolve around this form. When seriously explored, the short story seems to me the most difficult and disciplining form of prose writing extant. Whatever control and technique I may have I owe entirely to my training in this medium.

INTERVIEWER: What do you mean exactly by "control"?

CAPOTE: I mean maintaining a stylistic and emotional upper hand over your material. Call it precious and go to hell, but I believe a story can be wrecked by a faulty rhythm in a sentence —especially if it occurs toward the end—or a mistake in paragraphing, even punctuation. Henry James is the maestro of the semicolon. Hemingway is a first-rate paragrapher. From the point of view of ear, Virginia Woolf never wrote a bad sentence. I don't mean to imply that I successfully practice what I preach. I try, that's all.

INTERVIEWER: How does one arrive at short-story technique?

CAPOTE: Since each story presents its own technical problems, obviously one can't generalize about them on a two-times-two-equals-four basis. Finding the right form for your story is simply to realize the most *natural* way of telling the story. The test of whether or not a writer has divined the natural shape of his story is just this: after reading it, can you imagine it differently, or does it silence your imagination and seem to you absolute and final? As an orange is final. As an orange is something nature has made just right.

INTERVIEWER: Are there devices one can use in improving one's technique?

CAPOTE: Work is the only device I know of. Writing has laws of perspective, of light and shade, just as painting does, or music. If you are born knowing them, fine. If not, learn them. Then rearrange the rules to suit yourself. Even Joyce, our most extreme disregarder, was a superb craftsman; he could write *Ulysses because* he could write *Dubliners.* Too many writers seem to consider the writing of short stories as a kind of finger exercise. Well, in such cases, it is certainly only their fingers they are exercising. . . .

Frank O'Connor

THE PARIS REVIEW

INTERVIEWER: Why do you prefer the short story for your medium?

O'CONNOR: Because it's the nearest thing I know to lyric poetry —I wrote lyric poetry for a long time, then discovered that God had not intended me to be a lyric poet, and the nearest thing to that is the short story. A novel actually requires far more logic and far more knowledge of circumstances, whereas a short story can have the sort of detachment from circumstances that lyric poetry has.

INTERVIEWER: Faulkner has said, "Maybe every novelist wants to write poetry first, finds he can't, and then tries the short story, which is the most demanding form after poetry. And, failing at that, only then does he take up novel writing." What do you think about this?

O'CONNOR: I'd love to console myself, it's that neat—it sounds absolutely perfect except that it implies, as from a short-story writer, that the novel is just an easy sort of thing that you slide gently into, whereas, in fact, my own experience with the novel is that it was always too difficult for me to do. At least to do a novel like *Pride and Prejudice* requires something more than to be a failed B.A. or a failed poet or a failed short-story writer, or a failed anything else. Creating in the novel a sense of continuing life is the thing. We don't have that problem in the short story, where you merely suggest continuing life. In the novel, you have to create it, and that explains one of my quarrels with modern novels. Even a novel like *As I Lay Dying*, which I admire enormously, is not a novel at all, it's a short story. To me a novel is something that's built around the character of time, the nature of time, and the effects that time has on events and characters. When I see a novel that's supposed to take place in twenty-four hours, I just wonder why the man padded out the short story.

INTERVIEWER: Yeats said, "O'Connor is doing for Ireland what Chekhov did for Russia." What do you think of Chekhov?

O'CONNOR: Oh, naturally I admire Checkhov extravagantly, I think every short-story writer does. He's inimitable, a person to read and admire and worship—but never, never, never to imitate. He's got all the most extraordinary technical devices, and the moment you start imitating him without those technical devices, you fall into a sort of rambling narrative, as I think even a good story writer like Katherine Mansfield did. She sees that Chekhov apparently constructs a story without episodic interest, so she decides that if she constructs a story without episodic interest it will be equally good. It isn't. What she forgets is that Chekhov had a long career as a journalist, as a writer for comic magazines, writing squibs, writing vaudevilles, and he had learned the art very, very early of maintaining interest, of creating a bony structure. It's only concealed in the later work. They think they can do without that bony structure, but they're all wrong. . . .

INTERVIEWER: What about working habits? How do you start a story?

O'CONNOR: "Get black on white" used to be Maupassant's advice—that's what I always do. I don't give a hoot what the writing's like, I write any sort of rubbish which will cover the main outlines of the story, then I can begin to see it. When I write, when I draft a story, I never think of writing nice sentences about, "It was a nice August evening when Elizabeth Jane Moriarty was coming down the road." I just write roughly what happened, and then I'm able to see what the construction looks like. It's the design of the story which to me is most important, the thing that tells you there's a bad gap in the narrative here and you really ought to fill that up in some way or another. I'm always looking at the design of a story, not the treatment. Yesterday I was finishing off a piece about my friend A. E. Coppard, the greatest of all the English storytellers, who died about a fortnight ago. I was describing the way Coppard must have written these stories, going around with a notebook, recording what the lighting looked like, what that house looked like, and all the time using metaphor to suggest it to himself. "The road looked like a mad serpent going up the hill," or something of the kind, and "She said so-and-so, and the man in the pub said something else." After he had written them all out, he must have got the outline of his story, and he'd start working in all the details. Now, I could never do that at all. I've got to see what these people did, first of all, and *then* I start thinking of whether it was a nice August evening or a spring evening. I have to wait for the theme before I can do anything.

INTERVIEWER: Do you rewrite?

O'CONNOR: Endlessly, endlessly, endlessly. And keep on rewriting, and after it's published, and then after it's published in book form, I usually rewrite it again. I've rewritten versions of most of my early stories and one of these days, God help, I'll publish these as well.

INTERVIEWER: Do you keep notes as a source of supply for future stories?

O'CONNOR: Just notes of themes. If somebody tells me a good story, I'll write it down in my four lines; that is the secret of the theme. If you make the subject of a story twelve or fourteen lines, that's a treatment. You've already committed yourself to the sort of character, the sort of surroundings, and the moment you've committed yourself, the story is already written. It has ceased to be fluid, you can't design it any longer, you can't model it. So I always confine myself to my four lines. If it won't go into four, that means you haven't reduced it to its ultimate simplicity, reduced it to the fable. . . .

Vocabulary Study

The following vocabulary lists contain words which may be unfamiliar to the student. Not all of the difficult words are listed here, nor will all of the words that are listed be unknown to all students. The lists will serve, however, as beginnings for a study of the vocabulary in this text. Inasmuch as the definitions are intended as reading aids, they apply to words as used in the selections and are consequently not to be taken as complete definitions. Some of the allusions, too, are explained briefly.

Ugly Words – *J. Donald Adams* p. 2

conjure up   to make up; to imagine
nice-nellieism   a word that tries to be overly fastidious or too nice
nth degree   to an indefinite degree of power; extreme
stoutly homespun air   an air that is plain and unpretentious
ultimate in verbal absurdity   a word or expression as absurd or ridiculous as it is possible to be
euphony   pleasing sound
pestiferous   troublesome, annoying

Sound and Sense of Words – *John P. Sisk* p. 5

small-talk   mere conversation; talk to no special point
a dictionary approach to language   insistence upon precise dictionary definitions; use of the dictionary as the final authority for usage
a semantic problem   a problem involving meaning, a deeper and more complicated meaning than that presented by the simple definitions of the words
Semantics is concerned with what some call "the meaning of meaning."
in situ   Latin for "in its original place"
ecologist   one who studies that branch of biology dealing with organisms and their development

Eliot T. S. Eliot, poet, born in America; became a British subject (1888–1965)
The Waste Land, Murder in the Cathedral, and *The Cocktail Party* are among his better known works.

gestalt formula from gestalt psychology, which argues that something must be examined as a whole rather than as the sum of its parts.

hopelessly subjective completely unable to view anything except in terms of one's self

evocative potential the possible power to evoke something, in this case the power of words to evoke emotions, etc.

polyphiloprogenitive very productive of offspring

sapient wise. Often used ironically

sutler one who follows and supplies armies

Coleridge Samuel Taylor Coleridge, the English romantic poet (1772–1834)

Cullen Bryant William Cullen Bryant, the American poet (1794–1878)

incarnadine to make red

unambiguously mimetic mimicking in only one possible manner

multitudinous existing in a great multitude

Arthur Lovejoy American philosopher (d. 1963). *The Great Chain of Being* his best-known book

Wordsworth William Wordsworth (1770–1850), English poet; pioneer, with Coleridge, in the Romantic movement

Donne John Donne (1572–1631), English poet and clergyman

impregnated them with the garlic of huckstering filled the words with the air or flavor of the peddler or advertiser

neo-classical belonging to a revival of a classical style, as in poetry

systolic a shortening or contraction, as with the human heart. During the diastole the heart muscle relaxes and during the systole it contracts and pumps blood. Here the author is referring to a kind of cycle.

English: His Sisters, His Cousins, His Aunts – *Charlton Laird* p. 14

Venerable Bede a historian and scholar who wrote many works dealing with English history. Buried at Durham, England. (673–735)

obstreperous unruly, noisy, boisterous

dynastic wars wars to determine the succession to a throne

analogous corresponding in some particular; having similarity

etymological guess a guess or conclusion based on etymology, the study of the history of words

The Enrichment of the Language During the Renaissance – *Albert C. Baugh* p. 19

smelled too much of the lamp a reference to the lamp of the scholar or scribe, hence too pedantic, too scholarly

Restoration re-establishment of the monarchy in England in 1660

Renaissance revival of learning and art in Europe during the fourteenth, fifteenth, and sixteenth centuries

Romance languages any language derived from Low Latin: Portuguese, Catalan, Provençal, French, Rhaeto-Romanic, Italian, Romanian

Sir Thomas Elyot (1490?–1546) English diplomat, author, and lexicographer

Sir Thomas More (1478–1535) English statesman and author. Became saint

Sir John Cheke (1514–1557) Professor of Greek at Cambridge. Translator

Morning Exercises – *Robert M. Coates* p. 24

etymological etymology is the study of word origins, where words come from. It is the study of the history of words.

redundancy unnecessary to the meaning, as in "wet water" and "hungrily famished"

metaphorical folklore the expressions listed by Coates are kins of metaphors, in which the exact, literal definitions of the words will not give us the meaning intended. Folklore refers to the legends, the sayings, the customs of a people.

cadge here used to mean "beg"

simulate pretend, act like

enigma riddle; a baffling, puzzling statement

charade a game in which one has to guess a word or phrase that is acted out

concoct devise or plan
muddlement a muddle is a confused, uncertain, messy state.
Coates is here coining a word to describe a muddled state
totem an image, properly of an animal or natural object that is
thought to be in some way related to a family or tribe and
hence representative of it or standing for it
flauntingly in a conspicuous or defiant manner
synecdoche a kind of figure of speech in which a part stands
for the whole. "He's earning his bread" rather than "He's
earning his food," and "There are ten sails in the harbor"
rather than "There are ten ships in the harbor."

English Is a Queer Language – *Alice Hamilton, M.D.* p. 29

idiomatic something peculiar to a language, often having no
discernible connection to the language's grammar and sometimes even contradictory. Idiom, then, cannot be figured
out; it must be learned. The illustrations Dr. Hamilton
offers concerning the verb "go" are helpful.
ad infinitum without limit; endlessly

They Talk Past Each Other – *Irving Lee* p. 33

acrimonious bitter, angry
cipher a code, in this case the use of the initials "N.P." to indicate that no plates were to be made of the x-ray photo-
graphs
portent a kind of sign that warns or foretells
Hardy Thomas Hardy, English novelist and poet
Du Maurier George du Maurier, British artist and novelist
Black William Black, Scottish novelist and journalist
Gosse Edmund Gosse, English critic and student of Scandinavian languages
Howells William Dean Howells, American novelist and editor
lexicographical heresy a usage not according to the strict dictionary usage

About: New Words – *Martin Tolchin*   p. 44

lexicographer   one who compiles dictionaries
addenda   things added, usually in an appendix
etymology   the history of a word

The Freshman and His Dictionary – *Mitford M. Mathews*   p. 49

prescribe   order or direct
the Indo-European group   a family of languages including most spoken in or derived from Europe and many in southwestern Asia and India. The term is also used to label a hypothetical ancient language from which scholars believe the modern Indo-European languages to have been derived.
philology   the study of written texts in order to discover their meaning, authenticity, etc.
progenitor   ancestor
transliterate   to attempt to write or spell sounds in the characters of another language's alphabet. One example is the way we represent ancient Greek letters in the names of fraternities and sororities.
hybrid   anything of mixed origin; in this case, words put together from mixed sources
behoove   to be necessary or to be fitting and proper
cognate   related by family; having the same ancestor. English "apple" and German "apfel" are cognate words; French and Spanish are cognate languages
assiduous   diligent; done with attention

How To Read a Dictionary – *Mortimer Adler*   p. 56

edified   mentally improved
staid   quiet and serious; proper
sacerdotal   concerning priests; priestly
arbiter   a person who controls; an arbitrator
pedagogue   a teacher
glossary   lists and explanations of special words or special meanings of words
archaic   old-fashioned; antique

literary allusion   reference to something literary, usually to make a statement clearer or more interesting. "He was as stingy as Scrooge" is an example

stultify   cause to make foolish; make absurd

pedant   one who over-emphasizes book-learning, rules, regulations

inflection   the change in tone or pitch of the voice; the change of sound and hence form and spelling of words to show different functions, as "foot" to "feet," "swim" to "swam"

idiomatic   an accepted phrase or pattern often having a meaning different from the literal or grammatical meaning. It is idiomatic in English that although the sun rises it does not sit.

Sabotage in Springfield – *Wilson Follett*   p. 66

recondite   little known; out of the way

consummate   complete

puristical bigotry   last stronghold or fort of those who blindly and illogically hold to some standard of language purity

vestige of linguistic punctilio   remnant or remaining evidence of word-formality

syntax   rules for sentence-building

anomalous   irregular; different from normal

tacitly   understood without being said directly and explicitly

abrogation   repeal

George Ade   American humorist

jaded   worn, hackneyed, tired

neologism   new word coinage

succinct   brief and clear; terse

solecism   error in language

double approbation   dual approval

martinet   one who requires and strictly enforces discipline, perhaps over-strictly

egregiously overweighted   flagrantly padded

ephemeral   passing; temporary

But What's a Dictionary For? – *Bergen Evans*   p. 77

interpose   intrude, come between

extraneous   something that can be disposed of, done without

genus   family or class of things

inseminating scholars scholars who propagate ideas, cause others to follow

pervasively spreading throughout

unbuttoned gibberish incomprehensible, idiotic language or mere sound

cumbrous cumbersome, clumsy

abdicated its responsibilities avoided or given up doing what it was responsible for doing

cognizance recognition

proliferation extensive growth, reproduction

naive simple, unlettered, unsophisticated

fulminate roar and rant, argue loudly

Gobbledygook – *Stuart Chase* p. 98

pretentious showy, making claims to admiration

polysyllabic word with more than three syllables

Mr. Micawber a character in Charles Dickens' *David Copperfield*, noted for his optimism, for which he had no foundation whatever. Here we see an example of a fictional character who has had his name adopted by the language so that it is often used, even by those who know nothing of Dickens' book. An even better known example comes from Dickens' character Pickwick; so completely has he been adopted into the language that the dictionaries list not only the name of the character but the derived adjective, Pickwickian.

semantic noise semantics deals with the relationship between symbols, usually words, and what those symbols stand for; it is an attempt to study meaning. Semantic noise is somewhat analogous to the meaning of noise in electronics or a discussion of high fidelity systems. This kind of noise is a meaningless jumble of sound that interferes with or eliminates meaning.

tautologies needless repetition of words, as in "descend down." Some tautologies are part of the accepted idiom. The careful user of English who would never say "descend down" might well say "rise up"

pedagogue a teacher. The term is sometimes used in a pejorative, unfavorable sense, for the reasons cited by Chase

monograph a work written about a particular subject, usually quite specialized

cliché a trite, overworked expression
prolix long-winded, wordy
literati learned people

How to Write Like a Social Scientist – *Samuel T. Williamson* p. 109

burdocks weeds with prickly heads or burrs
lexicon vocabulary belonging to a particular class or subject
verbosity excess wordage
caste particular group
pedantic excessive show of learning
Choctaw American Indian tribe; hence pedantic Choctaw is showy and excessive display in a foreign and hence unknown tongue
initiates people familiar with, in this case, social science
guild society, group, club
eschew shun, avoid
parlay to bet an original amount and its winnings on a subsequent race; hence in this instance to build up

Can You Understand the Rules of Federal Prose? – *James R. Masterson and Wendell Brooks Phillips* p. 115

unremitting labor work that does not slacken or pause; constant labor
emmet archiac word for ant
derived by pure induction the logical process of the scientist, in which observations are made and, on the basis of the observations, conclusions drawn, like theories, principles, and laws, from which one can then deduce correct or logical behavior
obtuse dull, not very perceptive
innate capacity ability born in, natural, not learned or acquired
naive unsophisticated, unaffected
intellectualize your nominalism see discussion
attributive nouns words normally considered as nouns used as adjectives, as in the example "book composition"
lexicographers dictionary makers
pedants those who make excessive and ostentatious and needless show of learning

extreme duress extreme compulsion
erotic amatory, sexual

Our National Mania for Correctness – *Donald J. Lloyd* p. 129

lucid exposition something lucid is something clearly understood and clear; exposition is writing intended to explain, examine
convoluted twisted around, contorted
euphony pleasant sound
Somerset Maugham British writer, perhaps best known for his story *Rain*
the simple inanities of their objective tests something inane lacks significance or point; Lloyd is here saying that the kinds of multiple choice and true–false questions asked on objective tests are often pointless
lewd in the fourteenth century the word often meant "ignorant" or "common"
James Boswell author of a biography of Samuel Johnson
Johnson subject of Boswell's biography; compiler of what many consider to be the first dictionary in the modern sense. (1709–1784)
Samuel Pepys usually pronounced "peeps." Best known for his diary in which he made brilliant and often shocking observations on English society of his time. (1633–1703)
monomania a kind of mental derangement in which one becomes attached to one idea or group of ideas; an excessive interest in one thing
monolithic uniform, solidly consistent. A monolithic concentration on usage is an attention that had no other object
Jacques Barzun dean of the graduate school at Columbia, writer on various subjects, including language usage
Wilson Follett essayist. His essay in the *Atlantic* magazine started the controversy about the third edition of *Webster's Third New International Dictionary* when it appeared in 1961
Bernard De Voto American historian and writer. For many years he wrote "The Easy Chair" in *Harper's Magazine*, from which vantage point he lambasted various aspects of the American scene including what he saw as a language degeneration

Leonard Bloomfield, Robert Hall, and Charles Carpenter Fries
linguists; professional and scientific observers of the English
language

beat the old Adam   here Lloyd is making use of the Biblical
story of the Fall. The old Adam is the human tendency to
sin. Here Lloyd refers to the tendency to violate rules of
language usage

Wolfgang Langewiesche   a writer who usually concerns himself
with matters pertaining to aviation

a fine Chaucerian swing   Chaucer often constructed expressions
such as the one by Langewiesche; hence such an expression
is called "Chaucerian"

E. M. Forster   English novelist and critic

locution   a form of expression; a phrase

nominal turgidity   something turgid is distended and swollen;
hence as applied to language it means pompous and bom-
bastic or windy. Nominal is here used in its sense of something pertaining to names or nouns. As Lloyd goes on in
the next sentence, he complains that his friend uses lots of
names or nouns but few verbs; hence there is little life or
action in the writing.

pedagogue, pedagese   a pedagogue is a teacher; pedagese is a
coined word to label the kind of writing used by teachers,
in this case "convoluted" or "turgid"

lacunae   a lacuna is a blank space, something left out or omitted

a covert and pusillanimous means   one covered and hidden;
hence cowardly or weak

Clear Only If Known – *Edgar Dale*   p. 136

inept   said or done inappropriately; out of place
uninitiated   not familiar with the subject; not initiated
parsimony   exaggerated economy; stinginess
the wrong medium   the wrong means

Ladies' and Gentlemen's Guide to Modern English Usage – *James Thurber*   p. 142

morass   marsh, soft land
inveterate   long-established
rhetorically sound   able to use words effectively

hauteur   haughtiness of manner

imputing a suspicion   suggesting or accusing

tantamount   equivalent in meaning or effect

extenuation   act of excusing

purely hypothetical   completely made up; something thought up for the purpose of discussion or argument

Faulkner in the University – *Edited by Frederick L. Gwynn and Joseph L. Blotner*   p. 150

tory   one who is old-fashioned; one extremely conservative

Anderson   Sherwood Anderson, the American writer who influenced both Hemingway and Faulkner, among others. Perhaps best known for *Winesburg, Ohio*

Joyce   James Joyce, Irish writer, author of *Ulysses* and *Finnegan's Wake*

expiating her crime   making atonement for her crime

tour de force   an activity requiring unusual ingenuity; an ingenius job

Kilroy was here   during World War II American soldiers wrote the phrase on walls all over the world

Cockney ostler   a man from London's East End who took care of horses

immolated   sacrificed

puerile folly   childish, unthinking foolishness

prognostication   a forecast

Ernest Hemingway – *Harvey Breit*   p. 163

equivocally   doubtfully, uncertainly

Earl Sande   famous jockey

Johnny Vander Meer   baseball pitcher

Manassa Mauler   nickname of Jack Dempsey, heavyweight boxing champion, 1919–1926

Bimini   area near the Bahamas, where Hemingway fished in the 1950's

Jess Willard   heavyweight champion, 1915–1919

Walter Raleigh   English explorer, soldier, poet, who played a part in the settlement of Virginia and was beheaded by King James I.